100
essential
knitting
stitches

100
essential
knitting
stitches

SUSIE JOHNS

THE GUILD OF MASTER CRAFTSMAN PUBLICATIONS

Contents

Simple Stitches

Textured Stitches

Colourwork Stitches

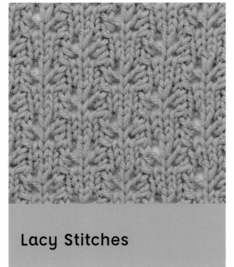

Lacy Stitches

Finishing Touches

Introduction

Knitting is such a simple pleasure – all you need is some needles and yarn and off you go. This book is suitable for all knitters: those who are picking up needles for the very first time, those who have tackled the basics and are ready to learn some additional skills, and those who have been knitting for years but are open to fresh ideas.

Divided into five sections, the first part of the book covers simple stitches, which is a good place to start if you are a beginner, as all but one of the stitches are made up of combinations of the two most basic stitches: knit and purl. The next section introduces more texture; some of these patterns are a little challenging and may seem fiddly at first, but the more you practise, the more effortless it will become. The stitches in the colourwork section are easier to achieve than you might think, as most of the patterns use only one colour at a time, with slipped stitches creating the designs: maximum effect for minimum effort. For the section on lacy stitches, the most complicated technique is not forming the stitches themselves but keeping count of the stitches and rows. Finally, a section on finishing touches offers a range of edgings, borders and embellishments to add a decorative touch to knitted projects.

You could carry on knitting swatches, collect these together and join them to make a patchwork blanket or throw, or you could choose a pattern for a plain sweater and substitute one or more of the stitches from this book to make a customised garment. You could knit one of the borders and add it to an existing garment. Or, if you have the confidence, you could design your own unique patterns, featuring some of these stitch patterns.

However you choose to use it, you will find that this book is the ideal reference for adding a touch of creativity to your knitting. With one hundred different stitches to choose from, there's bound to be something to help you to develop your own personal knitting style.

Difficulty ratings for stitches

Each stitch is rated with one to three blue dots, to denote degrees of difficulty. Those rated one are easy enough for a beginner; those rated two start to become a bit trickier; and three is reserved for the most difficult of stitches. None, however, is that difficult. Just follow the instructions and remember that practice makes perfect!

Tools and Materials

All you need to start knitting is a couple of basic items: needles and yarn. As you become more proficient, you will equip yourself with needles of different thicknesses and lengths and each time you complete a project, you will add the leftover yarn to your stash. When you are ready to tackle more complex projects, you will need some other tools: perhaps a couple of stitch holders and markers, a needle gauge and even a few cable needles.

Needles

Sizes and shapes

Some knitters – and I count myself among these – like knitting with thin needles and fine yarn. Others prefer something thick and chunky. Whatever your personal preference, you will need to have a selection of knitting needles in order to get the results you desire. Standard needles come in pairs, in a range of thicknesses and in a choice of lengths. You will need to have the right thickness to suit the yarn you are using and a suitable length for the size of knitted item. If you are making an adult-sized garment, the needles will need to be long enough to accommodate a large number of stitches, but if you are knitting for a baby, you might choose to use shorter needles as the number of stitches is likely to be a lot less.

If you are going to tackle a larger project such as a shawl, which requires a larger number of stitches, you may need to use a circular needle. These are designed for knitting in the round to produce seamless tubes of knitted fabric but they are also very useful for knitting back and forth in rows, particularly if there are lots of stitches involved, as the weight of the knitted fabric is distributed more evenly. And as the two needles are joined together with a flexible wire, it is impossible for one of the needles to go missing. If you find you prefer circular needles for most of your knitting needs, you may wish to invest in a set of interchangeable needles consisting of a number of pairs of needle tips in various thicknesses, and connecting wires in different lengths to suit different sized projects.

Also used for knitting in the round, you will encounter double-pointed needles, made from bamboo, wood, metal or plastic, and sold in sets of four or five. These are essential for knitting some of the stitch patterns in this book, such as a flat circle, hexagon or octagon, and invaluable for making items such as socks and seamless hats.

Another type of double-pointed needle is the cable needle, which tends to be much shorter, and is used for holding stitches while knitting cable patterns.

One more consideration is the needle tip: some needles are blunt and others are more tapered and sharp. When knitting some lace patterns, a sharp tip is an advantage, as it will more easily slip through several stitches at a time. If you are going to be making a lot of lacy patterns, you may wish to equip yourself with some particularly pointy needles.

Materials

Needles are manufactured in a variety of materials and you may develop a preference for one over another. It is a good idea to try a selection of different types, as some are better than others for working with certain yarns.

Metal

Having a shiny surface, metal is a good choice when knitting with hairy yarns such as wool or mohair. Thicker needles – more than 8mm in diameter – tend not to be available as they are too heavy. Look out for square metal needles, which differ from the more common cylindrical needles in that they have a faceted shape, are less strain on the hands, and help to maintain an even tension.

Plastic

Needles made from plastic are lightweight and inexpensive. You should choose plastic only for needles of 4mm or thicker, however, as thinner ones tend to bend or even snap. Plastic needles are a good choice for children learning to knit.

Bamboo

These are lightweight and flexible, and good for slippery yarns such as silk and bamboo. They are often recommended for arthritis sufferers. Try to avoid cheaper versions as they can be a bit splintery

Wood

Usually made from rosewood or ebony, wooden needles can be expensive. You may decide it's worth the expense, however, as they feel luxurious to use and can help to create an even tension.

Accessories

There are numerous gadgets available to knitters. Depending on the type of knitting you like to do, you will soon discover which of these you need and which you can easily do without.

Stitch holders

Used to keep sets of unworked stitches that you will return to later, these resemble large safety pins. For a small number of stitches, use a small safety pin.

Row counters

One version is a small cylinder, available in several sizes, that is slipped on to the end of a knitting needle. Other types are available, including ones that are worn around the neck like a pendant.

Stitch markers

Resembling paper clips, these are used to identify the beginning or end of a panel of stitches or the end of a round in circular knitting.

Cable needles

Used for holding stitches for a short time while working cable stitch patterns, the most common type is short and straight with a point at each end. Choose a size that is closest to the needles used for the main body of the knitting. Shaped needles are also available.

Pins

Use long pins with large heads to mark out tension samples and to pin pieces of knitted fabric together.

Point protectors

Place these on needle tips to help stop stitches from sliding off when not in use.

Needle gauge

This is used to measure double-pointed needles and circular needles that aren't marked with sizes.

Yarn bobbins

When working with two or more colours, these help to keep yarns neatly wound and less liable to tangle.

Tapestry needles

Blunt-tipped needles with a large eye are essential for sewing up and weaving in loose yarn ends.

Crochet hook

Keep one of these handy for picking up dropped stitches (see page 19).

Yarns

Knitting yarn is usually sold ready-wound into balls of a specific weight: grams or ounces. Some yarn is sold in hanks, ready for you to wind into a ball before you begin to knit. Most manufacturers provide useful information about the yarn on a label or ball band (see page 30). Read this carefully and keep as a reference, along with any spare yarn, which can be used for future repairs.

The projects in this book have all been knitted using Cascade Yarns 220 Superwash DK but yarns are available in different weights or thicknesses. Some are smooth and some textured. They are also made up from various different fibres, which makes a difference to the look and feel.

Wool
The most versatile and popular fibre, derived from sheep's fleece, wool has lots of elasticity and creates cosy, heat-retaining fabrics.

Merino wool
The merino sheep produces particularly soft wool and is a good choice for people who find other woollen yarns can irritate their skin.

Cashmere
Probably the most luxurious and expensive yarn, cashmere produces knitted fabrics that are soft and warm, yet lightweight.

Angora
Spun from the hair of Angora rabbits, this luxury yarn is incredibly soft. It is usually mixed with other fibres.

Alpaca
This soft, fairly hairy fibre from the alpaca, is one of the warmest natural fibres available. It is another yarn that's in the luxury category and is more expensive than most other natural yarns.

Mohair
This delicate yarn, from a breed of goat, is usually combined with other fibres such as nylon to add strength or wool to make it less irritating to the skin. The hairy texture means it is not really suitable for using with textured or lacy stitches as the stitch definition will be lost. It is definitely not suitable for baby clothes.

Silk
Silk yarn is light, strong and quite durable. It is often mixed with other fibres to make the yarn more affordable while remaining soft and luxurious.

Cotton
Cotton yarns are strong and practical, absorbing moisture and producing crisp fabrics with good stitch definition. Cotton fabrics are less stretchy than wool and it can be tricky to maintain an even tension when knitting.

Linen
Producing a good drape and a soft feel, linen is light and also very absorbent, making it a good choice for summer garments and household projects.

Bamboo
Like linen and cotton, bamboo yarns are cool and comfortable, with good absorbency. The knitted fabrics tend to drape well and are very durable. Pure bamboo yarns can be quite expensive but are often mixed with cotton fibres to reduce the price.

Soya or milk protein
Producing soft, smooth, absorbent yarns with a silky quality, soya or milk protein another fibre that is often combined with others, such as cotton or linen, to add softness. These fibres do not retain heat well and are better suited to summer knits.

Acrylic
Cheap to manufacture, this synthetic yarn is robust and moth-resistant and can be dyed in bright and sometimes luminous colours that would be difficult to create with natural fibres.

Nylon
Otherwise known as polyamide, this is a strong, lightweight and elastic fibre that is often added to sock yarns to increase strength and durability and to help prevent shrinkage and felting when washed.

Microfibre
This is one of the most popular and ubiquitous synthetic fibres in modern blended yarns as it is particularly efficient at holding other fibres together. It can also reduce the density of a yarn, making it lighter, adding texture and preventing pilling.

Basic Techniques

Holding the needles

There is more than one way to hold knitting needles and yarn and you will find what is right for you. Try following this basic advice and be prepared to adapt it slightly until you feel comfortable.

Hold one needle in your right hand, as if you were holding a pencil, with your thumb at the front; do the same with the other needle, in your left hand.

Holding the yarn in your right hand, pass it under your little finger, wrap it around the same finger, then over the third finger, under your middle finger and over your index finger. Use the index finger to manipulate the yarn and loop it around the tip of the right-hand needle, to make stitches. Having the yarn wrapped around the little finger helps to keep the tension even. If you find wrapping the yarn around the little finger awkward, try unwrapping it and, instead, just bend this finger so the yarn is trapped.

Making a slip knot

Before you start to knit, the first step is to create the first loop on your needle. Create a loop a short distance from the end of the yarn.

1 Take the yarn leading to the ball and pass a loop under and through the loop. Place this new loop over your knitting needle and pull both ends of the yarn to tighten the knot and shorten the loop.

2 The loop – or slip knot – should fit snugly on the needle so that it won't slip off but should be loose enough so that you can insert the other knitting needle into it.

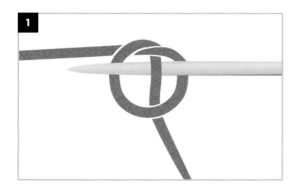

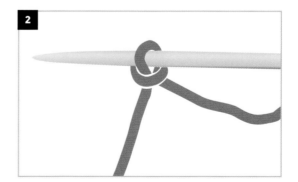

Casting on

Casting on refers to creating a number of stitches on which to work. There are several methods. Knitters tend to have a preference for one method over another, but it is important to learn a few different ones as they can be used for different reasons. The two-needle and cable methods create a firmer edge, while the thumb method creates an edge that is less well-defined and with more stretch.

Two-needle method

1 Create a slip knot on the left-hand needle to form the first stitch; pull it taut but not too tight. Insert the right-hand needle into this stitch from front to back, so that it crosses behind the left-hand needle. Wrap the working yarn anticlockwise around the point of the right needle.

2 Repeat the process described in step 1. Insert the right-hand needle into the stitch you just made, from front to back, so that it crosses behind the left-hand needle. Wrap the working yarn anticlockwise around the point of the right needle and pull the loop that is formed through the stitch, then forward..

3 Transfer the loop on to the tip of the left-hand needle to make another stitch. Repeat this process, each time inserting the right needle into the last stitch made on the left needle. Continue until you have the correct number of stitches.

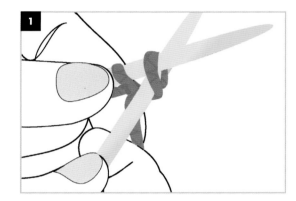

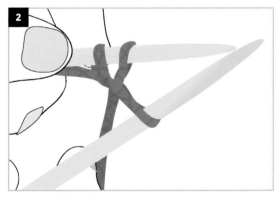

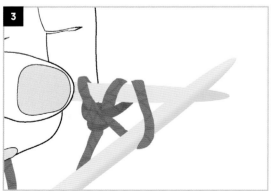

Cable method

Follow the instructions for the two-needle method (above) but after the initial two stitches, instead of inserting the right needle into the last stitch, insert it between the last two stitches. This creates a rope-like cast-on edge.

Thumb method

1 Leaving a long tail of yarn, make a slip knot on one knitting needle. You will need to estimate the length of the tail of yarn based on the width of the fabric you are going to create. The length of the yarn tail should be about three times this width.

2 Holding the needle in your right hand, wind the tail of yarn immediately next to the slip knot around your left thumb, from front to back. Insert the needle up through the loop of yarn on the thumb, then use your right forefinger to take the yarn over the point of the needle.

3 Pull a loop of yarn through to form the first stitch. Remove your left thumb from the yarn and tug on the yarn tail to secure the stitch.

Repeat the process until you have the required number of stitches on the needle.

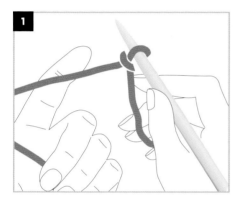
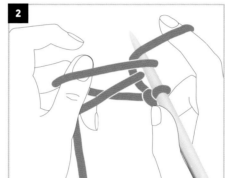
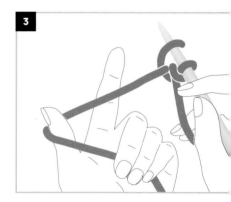

Basic Stitches

Knit stitch

1 With the working yarn at the back of the work, insert the tip of the right needle into the stitch on the left needle, upwards and from front to back; the right needle should cross behind the left needle. Wrap the working yarn anticlockwise around the tip of the right needle.

2 Using the right needle, pull the loop of the wrapped yarn through the original stitch, creating a new stitch.

3 Slide the original stitch off the left-hand needle; the new stitch will be on the right needle.

Purl stitch

1 With the working yarn at the front of the work, insert the tip of the right needle from right to left into the front loop of the first stitch. The right needle should be in front of the left needle. Wrap the working yarn anticlockwise around the tip of the right needle.

2 Using the right needle, pull the loop backwards and let the original stitch slide off the left needle.

3 The new stitch will now be on the right needle.

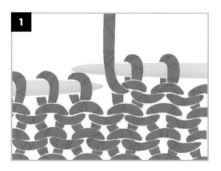

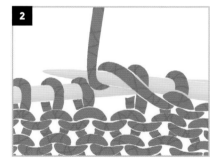

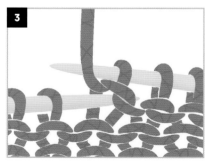

Increasing and decreasing

Techniques of increasing and decreasing serve various purposes: they help to shape a piece of knitted fabric and they can also create the decorative effects featured in lacy stitches and textured patterns.

Yarn forward increase
On a knit row:
To make a yarn forward increase on a knit row, bring the yarn to the front of the work, then take it over the right-hand needle and knit the stitch. By doing this, you will have created an extra loop between the stitches. This increase creates a visible hole in the fabric and is often used in lace patterns. This increase is abbreviated as yfwd (or sometimes as yf).

On a purl row:
Take the yarn over the right-hand needle to the back of the work, then under the needle to the front. The abbreviation in a written pattern is yrn (yarn around needle).

Note that sometimes the abbreviation yo is used as a catch-all term in both knit and purl rows, to indicate that you need to make a stitch by winding the yarn around the needle. In this case you will need to decide which method to use, remembering that you will need to create an extra stitch, not simply move the yarn from front to back or vice versa.

Working into the same stitch twice
The instruction kfb and pfb indicate that you need to work into the same stitch twice.

1 On a knit row:
Knit the next stitch but, before slipping it off the left needle, insert the right needle into the back loop and knit again.

2 On a purl row:
Purl the next stitch but, before slipping it off the needle, insert the needle into the back loop and purl again.

Make a stitch
The instruction M1 indicates that you should create a new stitch in between two stitches.

Having knitted or purled a stitch, use the tip of the right-hand needle to lift the strand of yarn lying in front of and just below the next stitch. Place this strand on the left-hand needle, then knit or purl into the back of this loop.

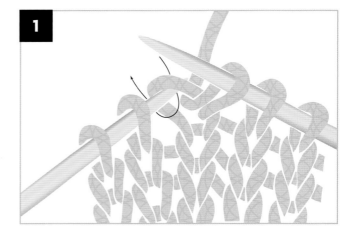

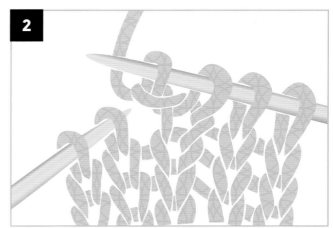

Slip stitch decrease

Slip the next stitch from the left-hand to the right-hand needle knitwise without knitting it, then knit the next stitch. Lift the slipped stitch over the knitted stitch and off the needle. The abbreviation is written as skpo (or sometimes as sl1, k1, psso).

Working two stitches together (k2tog or p2tog)

1 Insert the right needle into the next two stitches instead of just one.

2 Knit (or purl) them together as if they were one stitch.

Picking up dropped stitches

If you drop a stitch, try to pick it up immediately, before other stitches immediately below become unravelled. If the one on the row below has also dropped, use the right-hand needle to pick up both the stitch and the strand of yarn immediately below it. Insert the left-hand needle through the stitch and lift it over the strand of yarn. On a knit row, make sure you lift the stitch over the strand and drop it off at the back; on a purl row, drop the stitch off at the front.

If you have dropped a stitch and not noticed, it can form a ladder running in a line below the place where it was dropped. In this case, use a crochet hook to resolve the problem. Working from the front, identify the stitch loop at the base of the ladder, pick up the strand of yarn immediately above and pull it through the stitch loop to form a new stitch on that row. Repeat this process, working upwards until you reach the row you are currently working on.

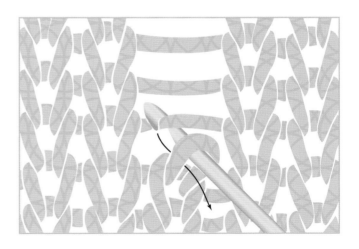

Joining in new yarns/ changing colours

Wherever possible, join in a new yarn at the beginning of a row. Leave a tail of yarn and loosely knot the tails of the new and old yarns together; these can be dealt with at the making-up stage. If you have to join in a new yarn in the middle of a row, simply pick up the new yarn, leaving a tail, and carry on knitting. Once you have completed a few rows, darn in the tails of the new and old yarns neatly at the back of the work (see page 22).

Casting off

There are two basic ways to cast off a stitch: one is knitwise and the other purlwise. You should, as a general rule, cast off in pattern: this means that you should cast off a knit stitch knitwise and a purl stitch purlwise.

Casting off knitwise
1 Knit the first two stitches. Using the tip of the left needle, lift the first stitch over the second and off the right needle.

2 Knit the next stitch and lift the previous stitch over this stitch and off the right-hand needle. Repeat until all stitches have been cast off.

Casting off purlwise
Follow the instructions for casting off knitwise but purl the stitches.

Tension

Tension – or gauge – is essential to a successful outcome. It refers to the number of stitches and rows required to fill a particular area of the knitted fabric: too many stitches and the work will be too dense and the fabric too firm; too few stitches and the work will be loose and the fabric liable to go baggy and stretch out of shape. Knit a tension sample: this will help to ensure that you achieve the right result. You may feel that this is a nuisance and you just want to get on with your knitting – but without doing so, your precious hours of knitting may result in a garment that is too large or too small and all that time will have been wasted.

Knitting a tension sample

Using the same yarn and needles as those recommended in the pattern, cast on a number of stitches: this will be the number given for the tension square plus a few more. Work in the specified stitch for the same number of rows, plus a few more. Block the square as you would for the finished project (see page 22).

Now use a ruler to measure out a 10cm (4in) square in the centre of your sample, marking the area with pins. Count the number of stitches in a row and the number of rows. If this number matches the tension given in the pattern, you can proceed, as the size and shape of the finished item should be correct. If, however, you have too many stitches and/or rows, your knitting is too tight and you should try again using a larger needle size. If you have too few stitches and/or rows, your knitting is too loose and you should try a smaller needle.

TIP The tension for a particular yarn is provided on the ball band (see page 30). However, this must be treated as a guide only, as your own tension might be different. Also, on the ball band, tension is usually provided for a sample knitted in stocking stitch; if you are going to use another stitch – such as one of the stitches from this book, especially if it is a textured or lacy stitch – it is likely to be very different.

Finishing and Joining

For a neat finish, you should use the correct techniques for shaping finished pieces of knitting, sewing pieces together and dealing with loose ends of yarn.

Darning in loose ends

Every piece of knitting will have at least two loose ends: one on the corner of the cast-on edge and one at the end of the cast-off edge. If you have joined in additional balls of yarn at any stage, you will also have other ends to deal with. These can be used for seaming: get into the habit of creating long tails if you know these will be used for this purpose. Otherwise, you will need to weave in these ends. To do this, thread each one in turn into a tapestry needle and weave it vertically or horizontally down the side of the work or through a row of stitches on the wrong side.

Blocking and pressing

This describes the process of shaping finished pieces of knitting to create the correct dimensions, to even out the stitches and, in the case of lacy stitches, open out the holes so the pattern is clearly defined.

Wet blocking
Dampen the pieces, either by spraying with water or by immersing in water. Gently squeeze out any excess water, then place on a suitable surface such as a board covered with a cloth, and use pins to hold the edges in place.

Pressing
Use a warm iron. Place the knitted piece on a suitable surface, lay a clean, damp cloth on top, and gently press with the iron. Gently stretch out the knitting to the desired measurements. Do not place the iron directly on to the knitted piece.

Steaming
Using an iron on a steam setting, place the knitted piece on a suitable surface and hover over it with the iron, applying steam, until the knitting relaxes. Do not place the iron directly on to the knitted piece. Pin the piece to the desired measurements and leave to dry.

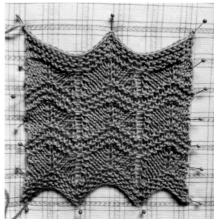

Seaming

If you are knitting a garment, the chances are that this will be done in several pieces that will need to be joined together. The method you choose will depend on whether you are joining two cast-off or cast-on edges, two side edges, straight edges, shaped edges, or a combination of any of these.

Joining cast-off edges

1 Place the two pieces to be joined right side up and with the edges touching. Thread a tapestry needle with a loose end of yarn and push the needle through the centre of the first stitch on one of the pieces, then in and out through the centres of two stitches on the opposite piece.

2 Now take the needle back over to the first piece, insert it where it previously came out and bring it out through the centre of the next stitch along. Repeat the process, alternating sides and inserting the needle under single stitches each time.

Joining side edges

There are several ways to do this. Two popular methods are described below.

Backstitch seam
Thread a tapestry needle with yarn and place the pieces to be joined right sides together, lining up the row ends. Work in backstitch, close to the edges, along the seam.

Mattress stitch
Almost invisible on the right side of the finished item, mattress stitch is the best technique to use when joining pieces of ribbing or stocking stitch.

1 Place the two pieces side by side, aligning the rows. Thread a needle with a long length of yarn and attach the end of the yarn to the lower corner of one of the pieces. Insert the needle from the front, through the centre of the first knit stitch and up through the centre of the corresponding stitch two rows above.

2 Take the needle across to the other piece and repeat the process.

3 Carry on in this way, working on alternate pieces, working upwards and creating strands of yarn between the two pieces, like rungs of a ladder. After a few rows, tug on the yarn to pull the edges together, then continue until the two pieces are joined.

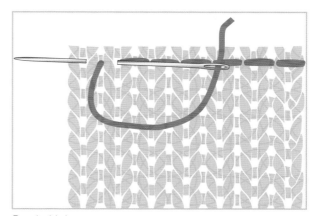

Backstitch seam

Mattress seam

Reading patterns

Knitting patterns are written in such a way that they may appear to be in a foreign language. This is because many of the instructions are abbreviated. If they weren't, the pattern might run on for many pages: the abbreviations keep things concise. A list of these abbreviations can be found below.

Before starting to knit, read through the entire pattern, to make sure you understand all the instructions. Note that instructions contained within brackets should be repeated; the number of repeats follows immediately after the brackets. Some pattern repeats are marked with an asterisk (*). Instructions following the asterisk need to be repeated and you will be told how many times to do this.

Abbreviations

alt	alternate	**p**	purl	**sl1**	slip one stitch
beg	beginning	**p2sso**	pass two slip stitches over	**sl2**	slip two stitches
C4B	cable four back			**(sl1) twice**	slip two stitches, one at a time
C4F	cable four front	**p2tog**	purl two stitches together		
dpns	double-pointed needles	**patt**	pattern	**st st**	stocking(ette) stitch
		pfb	purl into front and back of same stitch	**st(s)**	stitch(es)
foll	following			**tbl**	through back loop
inc	increase	**prev**	previous	**trs**	transfer
k	knit	**psso**	pass slipped stitch over	**WS**	wrong side (of work)
k2tog	knit two stitches together	**pwise**	purlwise	**yb**	yarn back
kfb	knit into front and back of same stitch	**rem**	remain(ing)	**yfwd**	yarn forward
		rep	repeat	**yo**	yarn over (to create an extra stitch)
kwise	knitwise	**RH**	right-hand		
LH	left-hand	**RS**	right side (of work)	**yrn**	yarn round needle
M1	make one stitch	**skpo**	slip one, knit one, pass slipped stitch over		
MB	make bobble				
MK	make knot	**ss**	slipstitch		

Needle sizes

Needle sizes differ between the UK and Canada, Europe, and the USA. If you have inherited some old needles from a relative, these may be sized according to the old British measurements that are no longer manufactured in the UK but are used in Canada; the UK has now adopted the metric system. These are shown in the table below, alongside metric and US sizes.

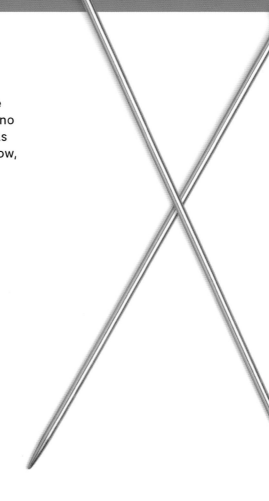

UK/Europe (mm)	old UK/Canada	USA
2	14	0
2.25	13	1
2.75	12	2
3	11	2-3
3.25	10	3
3.5	-	4
3.75	9	5
4	8	6
4.5	7	7
5	6	8
5.5	5	9
6	4	10
6.5	3	$10^{1}/_{2}$
7	2	$10^{1}/_{2}$
7.5	1	11
8	0	11
9	00	13
10	000	15

Standard yarn weights and tensions

Many yarns fall into specific categories when it comes to thicknesses and tension (gauge). The table below gives a guide to these standard weights and the recommended needle sizes:

yarn type (UK)	yarn type (USA)	tension: stitches x rows	needle size (UK)
Lace	Lace	30 x 36	3mm
4-ply	Fingering	28 x 36	3.25mm
Lightweight DK	Sport-weight	26 x 32	3.5mm
DK	DK	22 x 28	4mm
Aran	Worsted	18 x 24	5mm
Chunky	Chunky	14 x 19	6.5mm
Super Chunky	Bulky	9 x 12	10mm

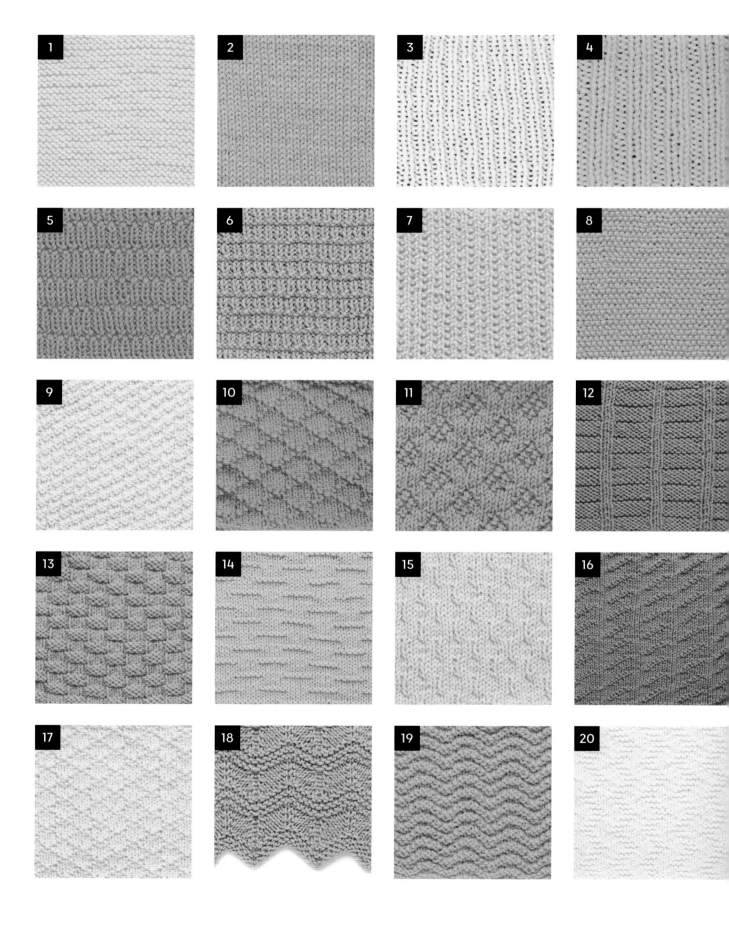

Simple Stitches

Front

Back

Garter Stitch

Garter stitch is the simplest of all stitches: you simply knit every row. The resulting fabric looks identical on both sides and lies flat, making it a good choice for baby clothes and blankets. Along with stocking stitch (see opposite) and single rib (see page 30), garter stitch is one of the basic three stitches that every knitter should learn before any others.

To work garter stitch:

Cast on any number of stitches.
Row 1: knit.

Repeat row 1 until the work is the desired length.

Yarn weights and substitutions
If you want to use a different yarn from the one suggested in a pattern, you need to bear in mind a few important points.
· to calculate quantities, look at the yardage/meterage on the ball band, not just the weight of the ball, as not all balls of the same weight have the same length of yarn.
· check the tension on the ball band to try and match the tension given in the pattern.
· look at the fibre content, bearing in mind that a pattern written for a wool yarn will be very different if knitted using a yarn made from different fibres.
· check the care instructions, as the pattern may be written for an easy-care garment that can be washed, so it may not be a good idea to choose a substitute yarn that is not machine washable.

TIP To create a neat edge, slip the first stitch on every row instead of knitting it. To make a slightly firmer fabric overall, knit into the back of every stitch: this is known as twisted garter stitch.

Stocking Stitch

Stocking stitch, also known as stockinette stitch or jersey stitch, combines the two basic stitches: knit and purl. When working on the right side, each row is completed in knit stitch; on the wrong side, each row is completed in purl. The result is the most basic and universally recognised knitted fabric, suitable for all kinds of garments, homewares, toys and just about anything you can create with needles and yarn. The right side is most commonly used, although the wrong side (known as reverse stocking stitch) can be used as the right side, if you wish. In written patterns, stocking stitch is often abbreviated to st st.

To work stocking stitch:

Cast on any number of stitches.

Row 1 knit.

Row 2: purl.

Rows 1 and 2 form the pattern; repeat these rows until the work is the desired length.

Blocking
Because of the difference in tension between knit stitches and purl stitches – knit stitches tend to be shorter and tighter than purl – stocking stitch has a tendency to curl around the edges. This can be remedied by blocking (see page 22), to even out the stitches.

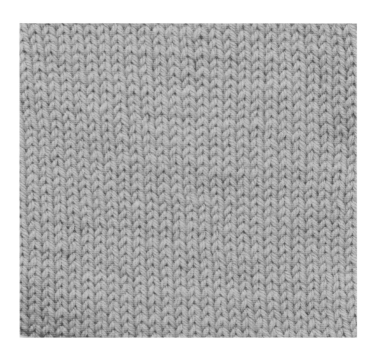

Front

Back

TIP To create a neat edge, slip the first stitch on every knit row instead of knitting it. On purl rows, slip the first stitch knitwise and knit the last stitch.

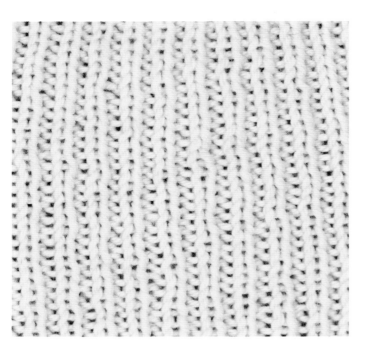

Single Rib

Single rib is a popular choice for the edges of garments – hems, cuffs and necklines – and for woolly hats, as the stretchy nature o the fabric helps to create a snug fit. Created by alternating knit and purl stitches along the row, it is straightforward to do. If you are a beginner, you may need a little time and practice to pass the yarn back and forth between the needles after every stitch, but it soon becomes second nature.

To work single rib on an even number of stitches:

Cast on an even number of stitches.
Row 1: *k1, p1; rep from * to end.

Repeat row 1 until the work is the desired length.

To work single rib on an uneven number of stitches:

Cast on an odd number of stitches.
Row 1 (RS): *k1, p1; rep from * to last st, k1.
Row 2: *p1, k1; rep from * to last st, p1.

TIP Remember: after a knit stitch, take the yarn to the front of the work, passing it between the two needles, ready to purl the next stitch. After a purl stitch, take the yarn to the back of the work, between the two needles, ready to knit the next stitch.

Ball bands

Check the ball band when buying yarns, as the information can be very useful. Typically, it will provide not only the name of the yarn and the fibre content but also the length of yarn in both metres and yards; washing instructions for the finished items, including washing temperatures and advice on whether or not to tumble dry or iron; a tension sample; and recommended needle (and crochet hook) sizes. The band will also be printed with the shade number and dye lot. What is a dye lot? Well, all yarn from the same batch will carry the same number. Different batches of dye can vary slightly so it is important that you use balls of yarn from the same batch within a single project, otherwise a variation of colour may show in the finished piece.

Double Rib

Ribbing is an important type of knitting, creating a fabric with sideways stretch. You have already been introduced to single rib (see opposite) but there are many variations of this basic stitch, double rib, or 2 x 2 rib, being one of them. If you are knitting a hat or a pair of socks, you are likely to need a ribbed fabric that will help these items to stretch and cling. You may also wish to create ribbed bands for the cuffs and lower edge of a jumper. Ribbing is often used for scarves, too.

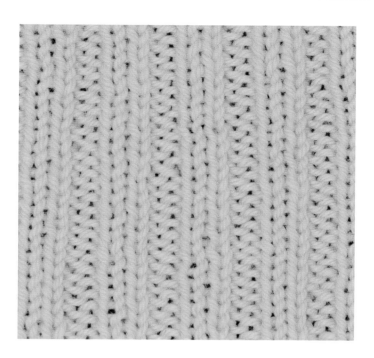

Double rib, as the name suggests, is formed by alternating two knit stitches and two purl stitches across the width of the fabric. On each row, to form the vertical lines of ribbing, purl the knit stitches of the previous row and knit the purl stitches.

To work double rib:

Cast on a multiple of four stitches.
Row 1: *k2, p2.

Row 1 forms the pattern; repeat this row until the work is the desired length.

TIP If you prefer, you can cast on a multiple of two stitches. In this case, where the total number of stitches is not wholly divisible by four, the double rib stitch pattern becomes a two-row repeat, where the second row is: *p2, k2; rep from * to end.

Broken Rib

Quick and easy to do, this stitch can be used in place of single rib on a garment or as the main fabric, offering plenty of stretch for a figure-hugging fit. The finished fabric lies flat and doesn't require blocking. It looks the same on both sides, and is ideal for a scarf.

To work broken rib:

Cast on an uneven number of stitches.
Row 1: k1, *p1, k1; rep from * to end.
Row 2: p1, *k1, p1; rep from * to end.
Rows 3–6: rep rows 1 and 2 twice more.
Row 7: as row 2.
Row 8: as row 1.
Rows 9–12: rep rows 7 and 8 twice more.

Rows 1–12 form the pattern; repeat these rows until the work is the desired length.

Banded Rib

Use this stitch in place of single rib or other ribbing stitches on cuffs, collars and welts, and for socks, wherever you need a stretchy ribbed fabric. It can also be used as a main fabric where some elasticity is desirable. It lies flat, and does not require blocking.

To work banded rib:

Cast on an uneven number of stitches.
Row 1 (WS): k1, *p1, k1; rep from * to end.
Row 2: p1, *k1, p1; rep from * to end.
Row 3: knit.
Row 4: p1, *k1, p1; rep from * to end

Rows 1–4 form the pattern; repeat these rows until the work is the desired length.

Seed Stitch

Seed stitch – or seeded rib – has two distinctly different sides. The right side has an appearance similar to moss stitch (page 34), with an allover texture, making it useful for sweaters, jackets and other garments as well as accessories such as hats. The other side resembles single rib and could be used for welts and cuffs, for the main part of a garment, or for boot cuffs or legwarmers. The fabric has a moderate lateral stretch. It has a slight tendency to curl at the side edges, but does not necessarily need to be blocked.

To work seed stitch:

Cast on a multiple of four stitches, plus three.
Row 1: p1, k1, *p3, k1; rep from * to last st, p1.
Row 2: k3, *p1, k3; rep from * to end.

Rows 1 and 2 form the stitch pattern; repeat these rows until the work is the desired length.

Front

Back

Fabric quality

When knitting any item, you need to decide if you want to create drape and fluidity or something more firm and stable. A loose-fitting jumper, a scarf or a soft blanket needs to have a bit of drape, while a fitted jacket, a bag or a cushion cover may require a firmer fabric with less stretch. Bear this in mind not only when choosing a suitable stitch but also the yarn and needle size for your project.

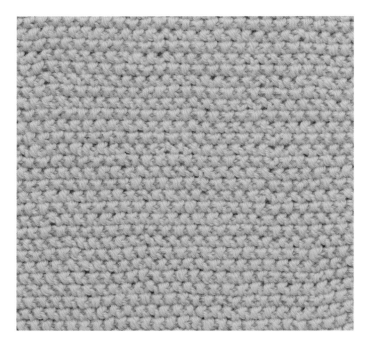

Front

Back

Moss Stitch

This stitch features alternating knit and purl stitches across each row. You purl the knit stitches and knit the purl stitches of the previous row, forming an even pattern of alternating stitch 'bumps'. This creates a two-sided fabric that has a slight two-way stretch but is essentially firm and hard-wearing. Attractive, useful and versatile, moss stitch is popular for all kinds of garments, accessories and homewares. It lies flat, so is ideal for borders, edgings, collars and cuffs, where you don't want the curl of a stocking stitch fabric or the stretch of ribbing.

To work moss stitch:

Moss stitch can be worked on any number of stitches; the pattern instructions vary slightly depending on whether you are working with an even or an odd number of stitches.

Cast on an even number of stitches.
Row 1: *k1, p1; rep from * to end.
Row 2: *p1, k1; rep from * to end.

Rows 1 and 2 form the pattern; repeat these rows until the work is the desired length.

Cast on an uneven number of stitches.
Row 1: *k1, p1; rep from * to last st, k1.

Row 1 forms the pattern; repeat this row until the work is the desired length.

This stitch pattern is known as moss stitch, or single moss stitch, in the UK and as seed stitch in the USA. In UK patterns, seed stitch differs from moss stitch and has a couple of variations, one of which appears on page 33. Where the term 'moss stitch' is used in US patterns, it is the equivalent of double moss stitch (see opposite) in the UK.

Double Moss Stitch

This stitch pattern is formed of two knit and two purl stitches across two rows, then a further two rows, offset from the first two. This creates an attractively textured two-sided fabric that is versatile and suited for all kinds of knits, including garments and accessories, blankets, throws, cushions and other homewares. Because it lies flat, it can also be used for borders, edgings, collars and cuffs.

To work double moss stitch:

Cast on a multiple of four stitches, plus two.
Row 1: *k2, p2; rep from * to last 2 sts, k2.
Row 2: *p2, k2; rep from * to last 2 sts, p2.
Row 3: as row 2.
Row 4: as row 1.

Rows 1–4 form the stitch pattern; repeat these rows until the work is the desired length.

Front

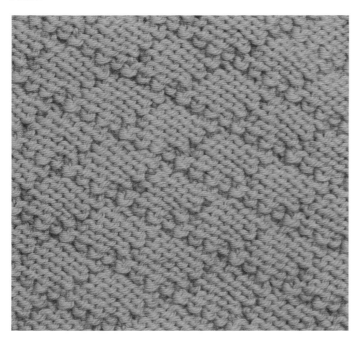

Back

Diamond Stitch

This stitch pattern features a neat trellis of diagonal ridges, forming diamond shapes on a stocking stitch background. It could be substituted in any pattern that uses stocking stitch where you would prefer a lightly textured effect instead of a plain fabric. Like stocking stitch, diamond stitch has a tendency to curl, so will benefit from being blocked (see page 22).

To work diamond stitch:

Cast on a multiple of eight stitches, plus one.
Row 1 (RS): k4, *p1, k7; rep from * to last 5 sts, p1, k4.
Row 2: p3, *k1, p1, k1, p5; rep from * to last 6 sts, k1, p1, k1, p3.
Row 3: k2, *p1, k3; rep from * to last 3 sts, p1, k2.
Row 4: p1, *k1, p5, k1, p1; rep from * to end.
Row 5: *p1, k7; rep from * to last st, p1.
Row 6: as row 4.
Row 7: as row 3.
Row 8: as row 2.

Rows 1–8 form the stitch pattern; repeat these rows until the work is the desired length.

Diamond Moss Stitch

This straightforward stitch makes a lightly textured fabric with an even allover pattern. The resulting fabric lies flat so you can choose not to block it – though blocking can help to define the diamond pattern, depending on the yarn used. It has an obvious right side and is a good choice for garments and items where the wrong side is not featured.

To work diamond moss stitch:

Cast on a multiple of ten stitches, plus seven.
Row 1 (RS): *(k3, p1) twice, k1, p1; rep from * to last 7 sts, k3, p1, k3.
Row 2: *(p3, k1) twice, p1, k1; rep from * to last 7 sts, p3, k1, p3.
Row 3: k2, p1, k1, p1, *(k3, p1) twice, k1, p1; rep from * to last 2 sts, k2.
Row 4: p2, k1, p1, k1, *(p3, k1) twice, p1, k1; rep from * to last 2 sts, p2.
Row 5: (k1, p1) 3 times, *(k2, p1) twice, (k1, p1) twice; rep from * to last st, k1.
Row 6: (p1, k1) 3 times, *(p2, k1) twice, (p1, k1) twice; rep from * to last st, p1.
Row 7: as row 3.
Row 8: as row 4.
Row 9: as row 1.
Row 10: as row 2.
Row 11: k3, p1, *k2, (p1, k1) twice, p1, k2, p1; rep from * to last 3 sts, k3.
Row 12: p3, k1, *p2, (k1, p1) twice, k1, p2, k1; rep from * to last 3 sts, p3.

Rows 1–12 form the stitch pattern; repeat these rows until the work is the desired length.

Front

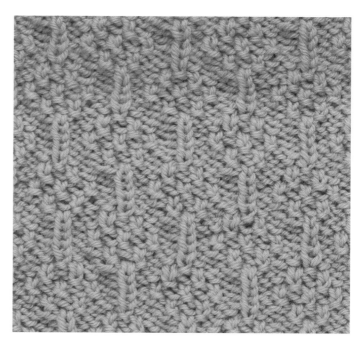

Back

TIP You will need to pay attention because of the large number of rows involved. Use a row counter to keep track, or lay a ruler or other straight edge on the printed pattern immediately above or below the row you are currently working on, to help avoid mistakes.

Front

Ladder Stitch

Vertical bands of stocking stitch resemble ladders, with garter stitch rungs. This stitch could easily replace plain stocking stitch in a pattern for a jumper, cardigan or other garment. The right and wrong sides of the fabric are distinctly different.

To work ladder stitch:

Cast on a multiple of nine stitches, plus two.
Row 1 (RS): p2, *k7, p2; rep from * to end.
Row 2: k2, *p7, k2; rep from * to end.
Row 3: as row 1.
Row 4: as row 2.
Row 5: purl.
Row 6: k2, *p7, k2; rep from * to end.
Row 7: p2, *k7, p2: rep from * to end.
Row 8: as row 6.
Row 9: as row 7.
Row 10: knit.

Rows 1–10 form the stitch pattern; repeat these rows until the work is the desired length.

Back

Basketweave Stitch

This stitch has a woven appearance that is evident on the right side of the fabric. It is not suitable for items where the wrong side would be visible, so use it for jumpers and accessories such as hats and bags.

To work basketweave stitch:

Cast on a multiple of eight stitches, plus three.
Row 1 (RS): knit.
Row 2: k4, p3, *k5, p3; rep from * to last 4 sts, k4.
Row 3: p4, k3, *p5, k3; rep from * to last 4 sts, p4.
Row 4: as row 2.
Row 5: knit.
Row 6: p3, *k5, p3; rep from * to end.
Row 7: k3, *p5, k3; rep from * to end.
Row 8: as row 6.

Rows 1–8 form the stitch pattern; repeat these rows until the work is the desired length.

Front

Back

Front

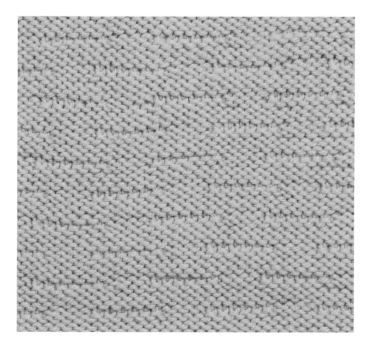

Back

Horizontal Dash Stitch

This is a subtly textured stitch that can be used in place of plain stocking stitch when knitting jumpers and similar items. The raised horizontal bars – or dashes – form an attractive allover pattern on a stocking stitch background. The front and back are different in appearance. The knitted fabric has a tendency to curl, so will need to be pressed or blocked.

To work horizontal dash stitch:

Cast on a multiple of ten stitches, plus six.
Row 1 (RS): p6, *k4, p6; rep from * to end.
Row 2: purl.
Row 3: knit.
Row 4: purl.
Row 5: p1, *k4, p6; rep from * to last 5 sts, k4, p1.
Row 6: purl.
Row 7: knit.
Row 8: purl.

Rows 1–8 form the stitch pattern; repeat these rows until the work is the desired length.

Vertical Dash Stitch

Here, short vertical bars, evenly spaced, sit proud on a reverse stocking stitch background. This stitch pattern looks effective on garments or as a cushion cover. You could choose to feature the reverse side instead, which is quite different in appearance and more subtly textured, like an undulating stocking stitch. The fabric, which curls slightly, will benefit from being blocked, using any of the methods described on page 22.

To work vertical dash stitch:

Cast on a multiple of six stitches, plus one.
Row 1 (RS): p3, k1, *p5, k1; rep from * to last 3 sts, p3.
Row 2: k3, p1, * k5, p1; rep from *to last 3 sts, k3.
Row 3: as row 1.
Row 4: as row 2.
Row 5: k1, *p5, k1; rep from * to end.
Row 6: p1, *k5, p1; rep from * to end.
Row 7: as row 5.
Row 8: as row 6.

Rows 1–8 form the stitch pattern; repeat these rows until the work is the desired length.

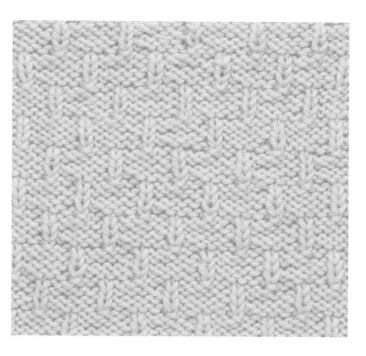

Front

Back

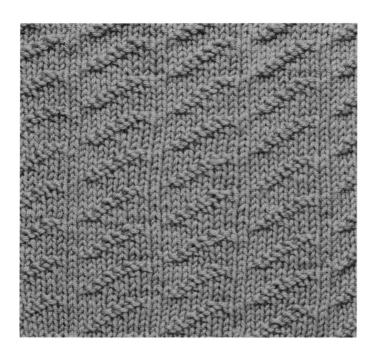

Caterpillar Stitch

This lightly textured stitch features diagonal 'dashes' formed from purl stitches that stand out from the stocking stitch background. It could be combined with other textured stitches to good effect on a jumper or other garment, or perhaps on a cushion cover.

To work caterpillar stitch:

Cast on a multiple of eight stitches, plus six.
Row 1 (RS): k4, p2, *k6, p2; rep from * to end.
Row 2: p1, k2, *p6, k2; rep from * to last 3 sts, p3.
Row 3: k2, p2, *k6, p2; rep from * to last 2 sts, k2.
Row 4: p3, k2, *p6, k2; rep from * to last st, p1.
Row 5: p2, *k6, p2; rep from * to last 4 sts, k4.
Row 6: purl.

Rows 1–6 form the stitch pattern; repeat these rows until the work is the desired length.

Lattice Stitch

This subtly textured stitch forms an attractive diamond lattice pattern suitable for all kinds of garments and home items, from sweaters to blankets. The front and back are different in appearance.

To work lattice stitch:

Cast on a multiple of six stitches, plus one.
Row 1 (RS): k3, *p1, k5; rep from * to last 4 sts, p1, k3.
Row 2: p2, *k1, p1, k1, p3; rep from * to last 5 sts, k1, p1, k1, p2.
Row 3: k1, *p1, k3, p1, k1; rep from * to end.
Row 4: k1, *p5, k1; rep from * to end.
Row 5: as row 3.
Row 6: as row 2.

Rows 1–6 form the stitch pattern; repeat these rows until the work is the desired length.

Ripple Stitch

There are many variations of textured stitches featuring waves or ripples. Using decreases and increases across the width of the fabric causes the stitches in the row to undulate. In this example, this is done over several rows of stocking stitch, with the shaping done on the knit rows, and these are interspersed with bands of garter stitch, creating wide, textured waves.

This stitch would look effective on a scarf or shawl that displays the zigzag edge to good advantage. It could also be used for a cushion cover or throw, among other items.

To work ripple stitch:

Cast on a multiple of eleven stitches.

Row 1 (WS): knit.
Rows 2, 3, 4 and 5: knit.
Row 6: *k2tog, k2, (kfb) twice, k3, skpo; rep from * to end.
Row 7: purl.
Row 8: as row 6.
Row 9: purl.
Row 10: as row 6.
Row 11: purl.
Row 12: as row 6.

Rows 1–12 form the stitch pattern; repeat these rows until the work is the desired length.

Front

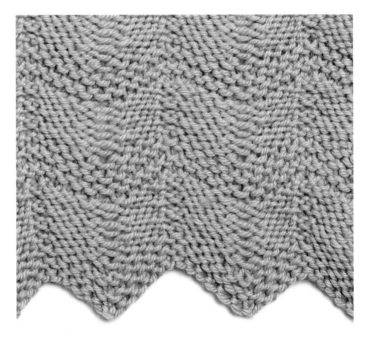

Back

TIP You don't have to stick to one colour: changing colours every few rows would produce a stripy zigzag effect that would show off this stitch well.

Front

Back

Horizontal Zigzag Stitch

This textured stitch forms raised garter stitch zigzag lines across the width of the fabric. It is double-sided, with a similar appearance on both front and back, and therefore a good choice for a cosy blanket or throw for the home, or for a scarf or wrap. The fabric lies flat and does not require blocking.

To work horizontal zigzag stitch:

Cast on a multiple of eight stitches, plus six.
Row 1 (RS): k6, *p2, k6; rep from * to end.
Row 2: k1, *p4, k4; rep from * to last 5 sts, p4, k1.
Row 3: p2, *k2, p2; rep from * to end.
Row 4: p1, k4, p4; rep from * to last 5 sts, k4, p1.
Row 5: k2, *p2, k6; rep from * to last 4 sts, p2, k2.
Row 6: p6, *k2, p6; rep from * to end.
Row 7: as row 4.
Row 8: k2, *p2, k2; rep from * to end.
Row 9: as row 2.
Row 10: p2, *k2, p6; rep from * to last 4 sts, k2, p2.

Rows 1–10 form the stitch pattern; repeat these rows until the work is the desired length.

Vertical Zigzag Stitch

This stitch forms a subtle zigzag design on the right side of the fabric and could be substituted for stocking stitch in patterns for jumpers, cardigans and other garments. It would also be effective as a cushion cover. The fabric has a tendency to curl and will therefore need to be blocked.

To work vertical zigzag stitch:

Cast on a multiple of six stitches.

Row 1 (RS): *k3, p3; rep from * to end.

Row 2: purl.

Row 3: p1, *k3, p3; rep from * to last 4 sts, k3, p1.

Row 4: purl.

Row 5: p2, *k3, p3; rep from * to last 4 sts, k3, p1.

Row 6: purl.

Row 7: *p3, k3; rep from * to end.

Row 8: purl.

Row 9: as row 5.

Row 10: purl.

Row 11: as row 3.

Row 12: purl.

Rows 1–12 form the stitch pattern; repeat these rows until the work is the desired length.

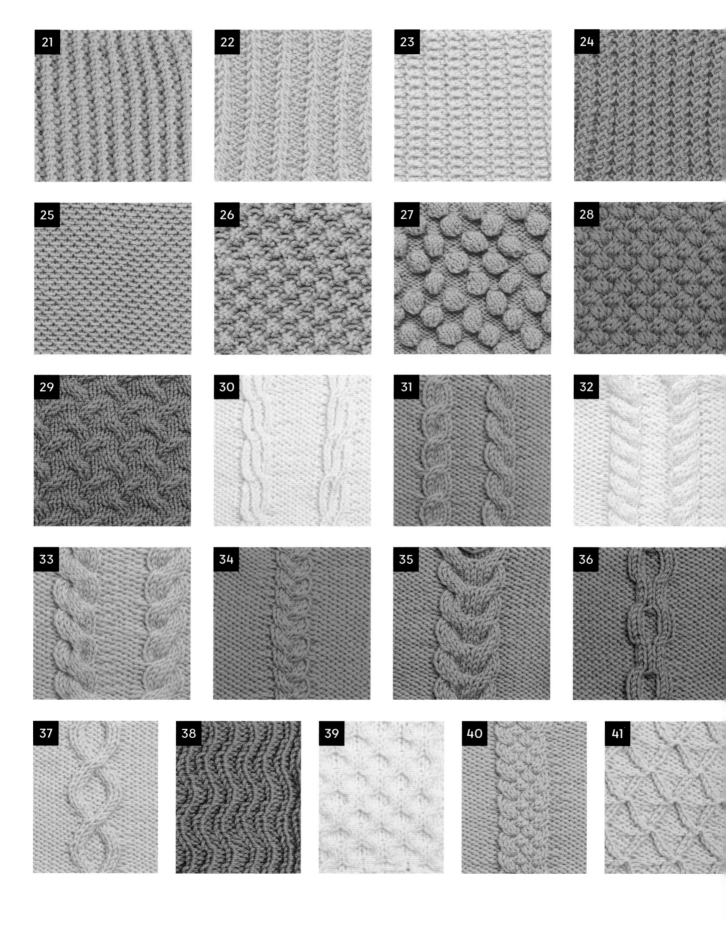

Textured Stitches

Blanket Rib

Easy to make, this thickly textured stitch is a good choice for blankets and throws and, because it has a similar appearance on both sides, excellent for scarves. It lies flat and doesn't curl, so is suitable for bath mats, table mats and runners too. The stitch is cleverly constructed by knitting twice into every stitch on odd-numbered rows, thus doubling the number of stitches, then alternatively knitting and purling pairs of stitches together on even-numbered rows to reduce the number of stitches to the original count and at the same time creating a thick ribbed effect.

Special abbreviation

k2tog tbl = knit 2 together through back loops Insert the right-hand needle into the back loop of the next two stitches and knit them both together.

To work blanket rib:

Cast on a multiple of two stitches, plus one.
Row 1 (RS): kfb in each st.
Row 2: k2tog, *p2tog, k2tog tbl; rep from * to end.

Rows 1 and 2 form the pattern; repeat these rows until the work is the desired length.

Feather Rib

Use this stitch in place of plainer ribbing when you want something a little more decorative. Both sides of the fabric are different but equally attractive, so it is a good choice for scarves, stoles and other accessories. Used as an allover stitch it would make a lovely skinny rib jumper, too.

To work feather rib:

Cast on a multiple of five stitches, plus two.
Row 1 (RS): p2, *yrn, k2tog tbl, k1, p2; rep from * to end.
Row 2: k2, *yfwd, k2tog tbl, p1, k2; rep from * to end.

Rows 1 and 2 form the pattern; repeat these rows until the work is the desired length.

Front

Back

TIP If you are using this stitch for ribbing, such as the hem or cuffs of a sweater, do not block it as this will affect the stretchiness. If you are using it as an allover stitch, however, you may wish to block it, to flatten it slightly and open it out, revealing more of the lacy pattern.

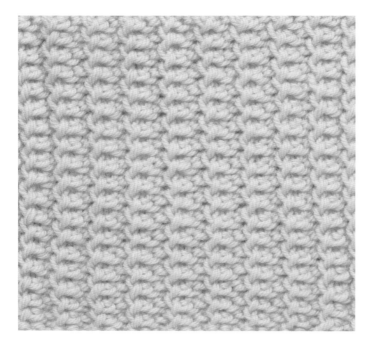

Front

Spiral Rib

Ribbed stitches can be very versatile. This one has good lateral stretch, is chunky and spongy in texture, lies flat and has an attractive reverse side, so will be useful for sweater welts as well as other items for which you would choose a ribbed fabric.

To work spiral rib:

Cast on a multiple of three stitches, plus one.
Row 1 (RS): p1, *k2, p1; rep from * to end.
Row 2: k1, *yfwd, k2, slip yfwd over 2 sts, k1; rep from * to end.

Rows 1 and 2 form the pattern; repeat these rows until the work is the desired length.

Back

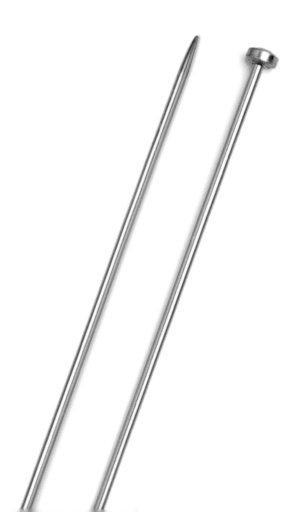

Corded Rib

There is no 'wrong' side to this stitch: the back and front are identical, making it ideal for items such as scarves and throws. It is firm and thickly textured with a little sideways stretch, and can be substituted for double ribbing on garments.

To work corded rib:

Cast on a multiple of four stitches.
Row 1: knit.
Row 2: k1, p2, *k2tog tbl, M1, p2; rep from * to last st, k1.
Row 3: k1, *k2tog tbl, M1, p2; rep from * to last 3 sts, k2tog tbl, M1, k1.

Rows 2 and 3 form the pattern; repeat these rows until the work is the desired length.

Honeycomb Stitch

This easy stitch forms a thick, firm fabric that lies flat and doesn't require blocking. Use it for homewares where the thickness will provide good insulation, such as a tea cosy or hot water bottle cover.

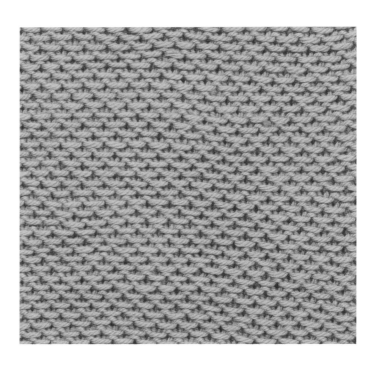

To work honeycomb stitch:

Cast on an uneven number of stitches.
Row 1: p1, *sl1 purlwise, p1; rep from * to end.
Row 2: purl.
Row 3: p2, *sl1 purlwise, p1; rep from * to last st, p1.
Row 4: purl.

Rows 1-4 form the pattern; repeat these rows until the work is the desired length.

Front

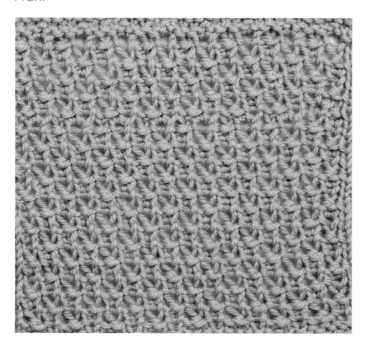

Back

Bramble Stitch

This stitch, also known as blackberry stitch, forms a thickly textured, knobbly fabric, perfect for a woolly hat, an old-fashioned tea cosy or a hot water bottle cover. It is also ideal for a winter jacket or cardigan and would look good combined with other textured stitches, including cables. Try not to work to a tight tension, as this will make it difficult to insert the needle into the stitches when working the p3tog (purl three stitches together).

To work bramble stitch:

Cast on a multiple of four stitches plus two.
Row 1 (RS): purl.
Row 2: k1, *(k1, p1, k1) into next st, p3tog; rep from * to last st, k1.
Row 3: purl.
Row 4: k1, *p3tog, (k1, p1, k1) into next st; rep from * to last st, k1.

Rows 1–4 form the pattern; repeat these rows until the work is the desired length.

Special abbreviations

p3tog = purl three stitches together
Do this by inserting the right-hand needle into the next three stitches, purlwise, and knitting them as one.

(k1, p1, k1) into next st
Knit into the next stitch, as normal, but do not slip it off the needle; instead, bring the yarn forward and purl into the same stitch, then take the yarn back and knit into it again; now slip the stitch off the left-hand needle, thereby increasing from one stitch to three.

Bobble Stitch

This highly textured stitch is flat on one side, with raised bobbles on the right side. The bobbles are otherwise known as clusters. Their construction may seem tricky at first but it is worth persevering with.

To work bobble stitch:

Cast on a multiple of six stitches plus five.
Row 1 (RS): purl.
Row 2: knit.
Row 3: *p5, MB; rep from * to last 5 sts, p5.
Row 4: knit.
Row 5: purl.
Row 6: knit.
Row 7: p2, *MB, p5; rep from * to last 3 sts, MB, p2.
Row 8: knit.

Rows 1–8 form the pattern; repeat these rows until the work measures the desired length.

Front

Back

Special abbreviations

MB = make bobble
With yarn in front, knit in next stitch but do not slip stitch off needle, (yfwd, k in same st) twice, turn and purl these 6 sts, turn and sl1, k5, turn and sl1, p5, turn and sl1, k5, turn and (p2tog) three times, turn and sl1, k2tog, psso.

Front

Back

Woven Cable Stitch

This basketweave fabric is relatively easy to achieve and has a simple allover cable pattern. You will need a cable needle for this. The fabric is very thick and spongy and has very little stretch. The back is neat.

To work woven cable stitch:

Cast on a multiple of four stitches.
Row 1 (RS): *C4F; rep to end of row.
Row 2: purl.
Row 3: k2, *C4B; rep from * to last 2 sts, k2.
Row 4: purl.

Rows 1–4 form the pattern; repeat these rows until the work is the desired length.

Special abbreviations

C4F = cable four front
Slip the next two stitches on to a cable needle and hold at the front of the work; knit the next two stitches from the left-hand needle then knit the stitches from the cable needle.

C4B = cable four back
As described above but this time hold the two stitches on the cable needle at the back of the work.

TIP Because the stitches are pulled tightly together, this forms a very dense fabric with a tight tension, so it is essential that you make a tension sample especially if you intend substituting it fo another stitch in a pattern.

Allover Cables

Cables are often used as a feature, as part of a design combining different stitch patterns or as a panel against a plain knit background. This cable pattern, however, is intended for larger areas, to create an allover texture, and would be a good choice for a cushion cover or a winter sweater.

To work cable fabric:

Cast on a multiple of six stitches.
Row 1 (RS): knit.
Row 2: purl.
Row 3: *k2, C4B; rep from * to end.
Row 4: purl.
Row 5: knit.
Row 6: purl.
Row 7: *C4F, k2; rep from * to end.
Row 8: purl.

Rows 1–8 form the pattern; repeat these rows until the work is the desired length.

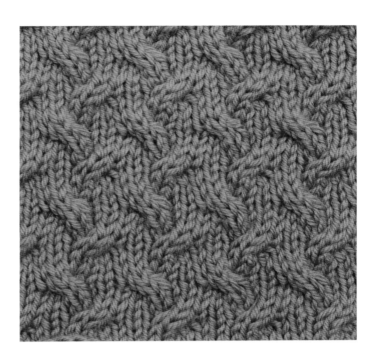

Front

Back

Special abbreviations

C4B = cable four back
Slip the next two stitches on to a cable needle and hold at the back of the work; knit the next two stitches from the left-hand needle then knit the stitches from the cable needle.

C4F = cable four front
Slip the next two stitches on to a cable needle and hold at the front of the work; knit the next two stitches from the left-hand needle then knit the stitches from the cable needle.

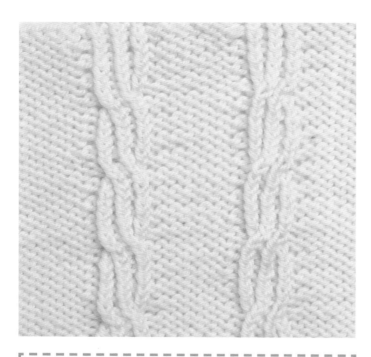

Triple-rib Cable

This simple five-stitch cable pattern is quite simple even if you are new to cabling. The pattern is given for two versions of the cable: one that twists to the right and one that twists to the left. It's up to you how many stitches to put between cables; in this sample, there are seven stitches between the two cables.

To work triple-rib cable:

Cast on five stitches, plus an even number of extra stitches for the reverse stocking stitch background.

Right twist version
Row 1 (RS): kb1, (p1, kb1) twice.
Row 2: pb1, (k1, pb1) twice.
Row 3: as row 1.
Row 4: as row 2.
Row 5: as row 1.
Row 6: as row 2.
Row 7: slip first 2 sts on to cable needle and hold at back of work, (kb1, p1, kb1) over next 3 sts, (p1, kb1) from cable needle.
Row 8: as row 2.
Row 9: as row 1.
Row 10: as row 2.
Row 11: as row 1.
Row 12: as row 2.
Row 13: as row 1.
Row 14: as row 2.

Left twist version
As above, apart from the following row:
Row 7: slip first 3 sts on to cable needle and hold at front of work, (kb1, p1) over next 2 sts, (kb1, p1, kb1) from cable needle.

Rows 1–14 form the pattern; repeat these rows until the work is the desired length.

Special abbreviations

kb1
Knit into the back of the next stitch.

pb1 = cable four front
Purl into the back of the next stitch.

TIP You could use this stitch pattern to create chunky ribbing on the hem and cuffs of a sweater, adding up to five stitches of reverse stocking stitch between each cable.

Four-stitch Cable

This basic four-stitch cable is a good pattern to start with if you are a cabling novice. Shown here are two versions, one that twists to the right and one that twists to the left. Here, an example of each is shown, with five stitches between the two. A skinny cable such as this can easily be added on either side of a wider cable pattern to create a larger overall design.

To work four-stitch cable:

Cast on four stitches, plus an even number of extra stitches for the reverse stocking stitch background.

Right-twisting four-stitch cable:
Row 1 (RS): k4.
Row 2: p4.
Row 3: k4.
Row 4: p4.
Row 5: C4B.
Row 6: p4.

Left-twisting four-stitch cable:
As above but on Row 5 work C4F (instead of C4B).

Rows 1–6 form the pattern; repeat these rows until the work is the desired length.

TIP The pattern is given for the cable only. To place the cable in the centre of a piece of work, you will need to create a ground of reverse stocking stitch on either side. Cast on an even number of stitches, allowing for the four stitches needed to make the cable. Divide the remaining stitches by two. Work in reverse stocking stitch up to the point where the cable begins, working in purl on the right side and knit on the wrong side.

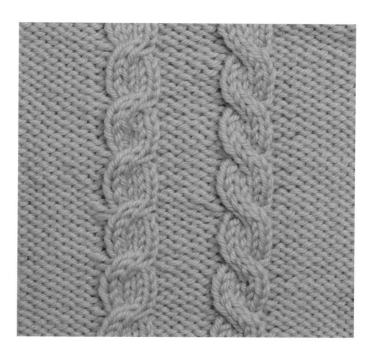

Front

Back

Special abbreviations

See Allover Cables, page 55, for abbreviations.

Six-stitch Cable

This medium-sized cable has a lovely rope-like twist. You can work this stitch so that it twists either to the right or the left – both versions are shown here. Like many other cable stitches, it is placed on a reverse stocking stitch ground, which shows it to its best advantage.

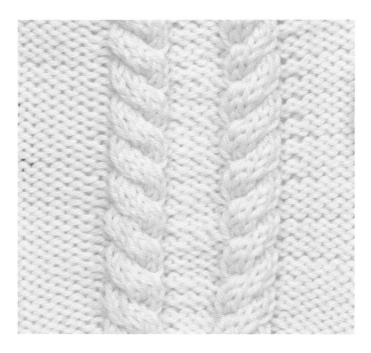

Front

Back

TIP When you add cables it will affect the tension, so you may need to cast on a few more stitches to compensate. Try adding half as many stitches as there are in the cables and be sure to knit a tension swatch to check before you embark on a big project.

To work six-stitch cable:

Cast on six stitches, plus an even number of extra stitches for the reverse stocking stitch background.

Left-leaning six-stitch cable:
Row 1 (RS): k6.
Row 2: p6.
Row 3: C6F.
Row 4: p6.

Right-leaning six-stitch cable:
As above but on Row 5 work C6B (instead of C6F).

Rows 1–4 form the pattern; repeat these rows until the work is the desired length.

Special abbreviations

C6F = cable six front
Cable six front is worked over six stitches; the cables lean to the left. Slip three stitches purlwise on to a cable needle, place the cable needle at the front of the work, knit the next three stitches from the left-hand needle then knit the three stitches from the cable needle.

C6B = cable six back
Cable six back is worked in a similar way to cable six front but the cable needle is placed at the back of the work and the cables lean to the right.

Cast on six stitches, plus an even number of extra stitches for the reverse stocking stitch background.

Eight-stitch Cable

This distinctive cable pattern with either a right-leaning twist or a left-leaning twist forms a thick band constructed from eight stitches on a reverse stocking stitch ground. Repeat multiple times over the body of a sweater, or use just one or two repeats as part of a complex design of several different stitches.

To work an eight-stitch cable:

Cast on eight stitches, plus an even number of extra stitches for the reverse stocking stitch background.

Right-leaning eight-stitch cable:
Row 1 (RS): k8.
Row 2: p8.
Row 3: C8B.
Row 4: p8.
Row 5: k8.
Row 6: p8.

Left-leaning eight-stitch cable:
As above but on Row 3 work C8F (instead of C8B).

Rows 1–6 form the pattern; repeat these rows until the work is the desired length.

Front

Back

Special abbreviations

C8B = cable eight back
Transfer the next four stitches purlwise on to a cable needle and hold at the back of the work, knit the next four stitches from the left-hand needle then knit the four stitches from the cable needle.

C8F = cable eight front
Cable eight front is worked in a similar way to cable eight back but the cable needle is placed at the front of the work.

TIP Use a cable needle that is the same size as the needles used for the pattern. If you don't have one exactly the same size, use one slightly larger – but not too large, or the stitches may become stretched.

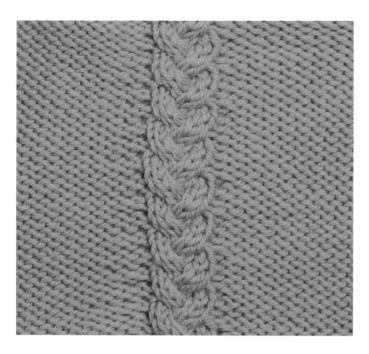

Front

Back

Six-stitch Plait

This stitch pattern forms a fairly narrow neat plait that can be repeated across the width of a piece of knitting such as the front of a sweater, or incorporated into a design by combining it with other cable stitches or textured patterns.

To work a six-stitch plait:

Cast on six stitches, plus an even number of extra stitches for the reverse stocking stitch background.

Row 1 (RS): C4F, k2.
Row 2: p6.
Row 3: k2, C4B.
Row 4: p6.

Rows 1–4 form the pattern; repeat these rows until the work is the desired length.

Special abbreviations

C4F = cable four front

Double Cable

This stitch pattern, worked over 12 stitches, creates a wide symmetrical band that would make a good centre piece in a cable knit design with narrower bands, such as a four-stitch cable, on either side. The Y-shape branching effect of the double cable resembles a pair of horns, and this pattern is sometimes called 'staghorn' cable.

To work an upwards-facing double cable:

Cast on 12 stitches, plus an even number of extra stitches for the reverse stocking stitch background.

Row 1 (RS): k12.
Row 2: p12.
Row 3: C6B, C6F.
Row 4: p12.
Row 5: k12.
Row 6: p12.
Row 7: k12.
Row 8: p12.

Rows 1–8 form the pattern; repeat these rows until the work is the desired length.

Special abbreviations

C6B = cable six back

C6F = cable six front

Front

Back

TIP Change the direction of the cable by changing the instruction in row 3 from C6B, C6F to C6F, C6B.

Front

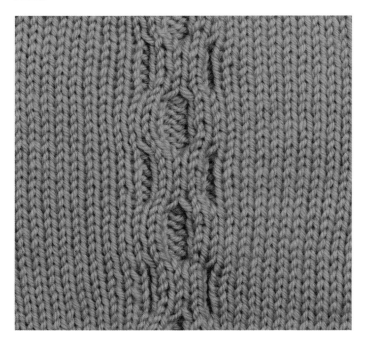

Back

Round Cable

This versatile stitch pattern produces a medium-width cabled band with a pattern of joined rings. It could be used in the centre of a design or on either side of a central feature.

To work round cable:

Cast on eight stitches, plus an even number of extra stitches for the reverse stocking stitch background.

Row 1 (RS): p2, k4, p2.
Row 2: k2, p4, k2.
Row 3: as row 1.
Row 4: as row 2.
Row 5: T4B, T4F.
Row 6: p2, k4, p2.
Row 7: k2, p4, k2.
Row 8: as row 6.
Row 9: as row 7.
Row 10: as row 6.
Row 11: T4F, T4B.
Row 12: k2, p4, k2.

Rows 1–12 form the pattern; repeat these rows until the work is the desired length.

Special abbreviations

T4B = twist four back
Slip the next two stitches purlwise on to a cable needle and hold at the back of the work, knit the next two stitches from the left-hand needle then purl the two stitches from the cable needle.

T4F = twist four front
Slip the next two stitches on to a cable needle and hold at the front of the work, purl the next two stitches then knit the stitches from the cable needle.

Chain Cable

This cable, worked over nine stitches, twists to the right and resembles a length of chain.

To work chain cable:

Cast on nine stitches, plus an even number of extra stitches for the reverse stocking stitch background.

Row 1 (RS): p2, T5R, p2.
Row 2: k2, p2, k1, p2, k2.
Row 3: p1, T3B, p1, T3F, p1.
Row 4: k1, p2, k3, p2, k1.
Row 5: T3B, p3, T3F.
Row 6: p2, k5, p2.
Row 7: k2, p5, k2.
Row 8: as row 6.
Row 9: T3F, p3, T3B.
Row 10: as row 4.
Row 11: p1, T3F, p1, T3B, p1.
Row 12: as row 2.

Rows 1–12 form the pattern; repeat these rows until the work is the desired length.

Special abbreviations

T5R = twist five right
Slip the next three stitches purlwise on to a cable needle and hold at the back of the work, knit the next two stitches from the left-hand needle then work (p1, k2) from the cable needle.

T3B = twist three back
Slip the next stitch on to a cable needle and hold at the back of the work, knit the next two stitches then purl the stitch from the cable needle.

T3F = twist three front
Slip the next two stitches on to a cable needle, hold at the front of the work, purl next stitch and knit the two stitches from the cable needle.

Front

Back

Wave Ribbing

This quirky stitch produces a wavy ribbing with the lateral stretch of a conventional ribbed fabric. It would look good as an allover pattern on a skinny jumper, or could be used to make a pair of legwarmers, wristwarmers or a beanie hat. The cable twist does not require a cable needle.

To work wave ribbing:

Cast on a multiple of three stitches, plus an even number of extra stitches if you are adding a reverse stocking stitch background. (Instructions are given for the wave ribbing only.)

Row 1 (RS): *p1, CR2R; rep from * to end.
Row 2: *k1, p1, k1; rep from * to end.
Row 3: *CR2R, p1; rep from * to end.
Row 4: *k2, p1; rep from * to end.
Row 5: *k1, p2; rep from * to end.
Row 6: as row 4.
Row 7: *CR2L, p1; rep from * to end.
Row 8: as row 2.
Row 9: *p1, CR2L; rep from * to end.
Row 10: *p1, k2; rep from * to end.
Row 11: *p2, k1; rep from * to end.
Row 12: as row 10.

Rows 1–12 form the pattern; repeat these rows until the work is the desired length.

Special abbreviations

CR2R
Miss the first stitch on the left-hand needle, knit the second stitch through the front loop but do not drop it off the needle; purl the first stitch, then drop both stitches together.

CR2L
Miss the first stitch and purl through the back loop of the second stitch by taking the right-hand needle behind the first stitch, then knit the first stitch and drop both stitches together.

TIP Working this stitch pattern may seem a little awkward at first, especially knitting stitches through either the back or front loop, manoeuvring the left-hand needle around the unworked stitch. Make sure you take the yarn to the back before knitting a stitch and to the front before purling or you might inadvertently create extra stitches.

Honeycomb Cable

This fairly straightforward cable pattern can be used as an allover pattern, repeated across the whole width of the fabric, or as a panel of various widths to be incorporated into a cable design with other stitch patterns. The example shown here is worked over 24 stitches on a background of reverse stocking stitch.

To work honeycomb cable:

Cast on a multiple of eight stitches, plus an even number of extra stitches if you are adding a reverse stocking stitch background. (Instructions are given for the honeycomb cable only.)

Row 1 (RS): *C4B, C4F; rep from * to end.

Row 2: purl.

Row 3: knit.

Row 4: purl.

Row 5: *C4F, C4B; rep from * to end.

Row 6: purl.

Row 7: knit.

Row 8: purl

Rows 1–8 form the pattern; repeat these rows until the work is the desired length.

Special abbreviations

C4B = cable four back

C4F = cable four front

Front

Back

TIP Remember when creating cable panels on a reverse stocking stitch background to work in purl on right-side rows, either side of the cable panel, and in knit on wrong side rows.

Front

Back

Braided Cable

This complex plait is not as difficult to knit as it might appear. It can be incorporated into a multi-cable pattern or used as a feature on a smaller item such as a pair of mittens or fingerless gloves.

To work braided cable:

Cast on ten stitches, plus extra stitches for the reverse stocking stitch background.

Row 1 (WS): purl.
Row 2: k2, (C4F) twice.
Row 3: purl.
Row 4: (C4B) twice, k2.

Rows 1–4 form the pattern; repeat these rows until the work is the desired length.

TIP If stitches tend to fall off your cable needle, it is probably due to using a cable needle that is too thin. Try to match the size of your cable needle as closely as possible to the needles used for the rest of the work. Cable needles are often sold in sets of two or three, giving you a choice: choose a slightly larger needle rather than a smaller one if you can't obtain an exact match.

Smocking Stitch

This unusual stitch creates a firm yet flexible fabric. Use it for the yoke of a sweater or a child's dress, or for homewares such as hot water bottle covers, tea cosies or cushions.

To work smocking stitch:

Cast on a multiple of eight stitches, plus seven.

Row 1 (RS): p1, k1, *p3, k1; rep from * to last st, p1.

Row 2: k1, p1, *k3, p1; rep from * to last st, k1.

Row 3: p1, wrap 5, *p3, wrap 5; rep from * to last st, p1.

Row 4: as row 2.

Row 5: as row 1.

Row 6: as row 2.

Row 7: as row 1.

Row 8: as row 2.

Row 9: p1, k1, p3, *wrap 5, p3; rep from * to last 2 sts, k1, p1.

Row 10: as row 2.

Row 11: as row 1.

Row 12: as row 2.

Rows 1–12 form the pattern; repeat these rows until the work is the desired length.

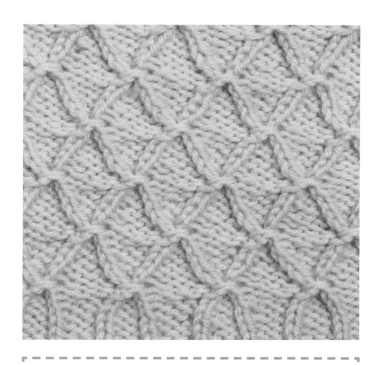

Special abbreviations

wrap 5
Slip the next five stitches on to a cable needle and hold at the front of the work then wrap the yarn twice, anticlockwise, around these five stitches, ending with the yarn at the back. Work (k1, p3, k1) into the stitches on the cable needle.

TIP The unusual construction of this stitch makes it a challenge even for experienced knitters. Bear in mind that when you work the 'wrap 5' instruction, you are tying five stitches together, which creates the smocking effect shown in the example above. Try to do this as evenly as possible for a neat result.

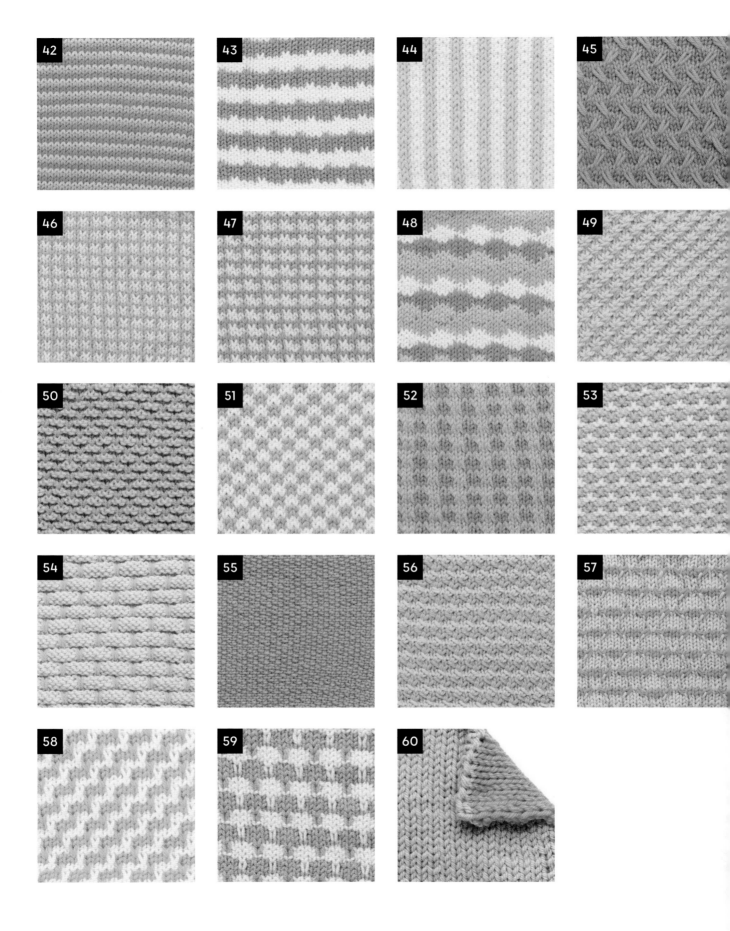

Colourwork Stitches

Front

Back

Single-row Stripes

This stocking stitch fabric features single-row stripes in three colours. It is a particularly good choice for small-scale striped projects such as dolls' clothes and baby garments. Bear in mind that, as yarn not in use is carried up the sides of the work, these edges will need to be finished or hidden within seams.

To work single-row stripes:

Use yarn in three colours, A, B and C.

Cast on any number of stitches.
Row 1: using yarn A, knit.
Row 2: do not cut yarn A but join in B; using B, purl.
Row 3: do not cut yarn B but join in C; using C, knit.
Row 4: using A, purl.
Row 5: using B, knit.
Row 6: using C, purl.
Row 7: using A, knit.
Row 8: using B, purl.
Row 9: using C, knit.

Rows 4–9 form the pattern; repeat these rows until the work is the desired length.

TIP Where you are instructed to slip one stitch, (sl1), do this purlwise: in other words, insert the needle into the next stitch as if you were going to purl it, but slip it off the left-hand needle and on to the right, instead.

Broken Stripes

This stitch creates a firm fabric with a definite right and wrong side. Use it for garments where the reverse will not show and for homewares such as cushions. You need to use at least two contrasting colours; carry the colour not in use loosely up the side of the work.

To work broken stripes:
Use yarn in two colours, A and B.

Cast on a multiple of four stitches plus two.
Row 1 (RS): using yarn A, knit.
Row 2: using yarn A, purl.
Row 3: as row 1.
Row 4: as row 2.
Row 5: using yarn B, k2, *sl1, k3; rep from * to end.
Row 6: using yarn B, purl.
Row 7: using yarn B, knit.
Row 8: using yarn B, purl.
Row 9: using yarn A, k4, *sl1, k3; rep from * to last 2 sts, sl1, k1.

Rows 2–9 form the pattern; repeat these rows until the work is the desired length.

Front

Back

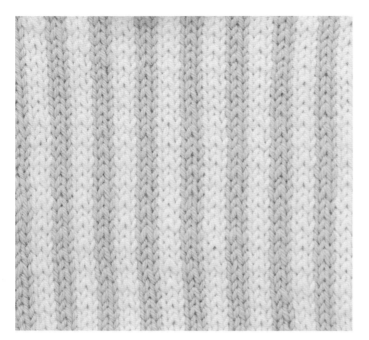

Front

Vertical Stripes

This stitch is not suitable for items where the wrong side is visible. However, it creates a thick, firm fabric excellent for items such as tea cosies and hot water bottle covers, where it provides good insulation. It is also good for bags that are to be lined, or for cushion covers, where the wrong side is on the inside and cannot be seen.

To work vertical stripes:

Use yarn in two colours, A and B.

Cast on a multiple of four stitches, using yarn A.
Row 1 (RS): using yarn A, knit.
Row 2: using yarn A, purl.
Row 3: using yarn B, k3, sl2, *k2, sl2; rep from * to last 3 sts, k3.
Row 4: using yarn B, p3, sl2 *p2, sl2; rep from * to last 3 sts, p3.
Row 5: using yarn A, k1, sl2, *k2, sl2; rep from * to last st, k1.
Row 6: using yarn A, p1, sl2, *p2, sl2; rep from * to last st, p1.

Rows 3–6 form the pattern; repeat these rows until the work is the desired length.

Back

TIP As yarns are stranded across the back of the work, take extra care to maintain an even tension or the fabric might become puckered.

Special abbreviations

sl2: slip the next two stitches with the yarn at the back of the work on all odd-numbered rows and with the yarn at the front of the work on all even-numbered rows. Note that all slip stitches should be slipped purlwise.

Vertical Chevron Stitch

This stitch uses two contrasting colours, A and B; it also requires a cable needle to produce the slanted stitches that form the vertical chevron pattern. Use it for projects where a fairly thick, firm, medium-textured fabric is desirable.

To work vertical chevron stitch:

Use yarn in two colours, A and B.

Cast on a multiple of four stitches, plus one, using yarn A.
Row 1 (RS): using A, k1, sl1, k3; rep from * to end.
Row 2: using A, *p3, sl1; rep from * to last st, p1.
Row 3: using B, k1, *c3L, k1; rep from * to end.
Row 4: using B, purl.
Row 5: using A, k5, *sl1, k3; rep from * to end.
Row 6: using A, *p3, sl1; rep from * to last 5 sts, p5.
Row 7: using B, k3, *c3R, k1; rep from * to last 2 sts, k2.
Row 8: using B, purl.

Rows 1–8 form the pattern; repeat these rows until the work is the desired length.

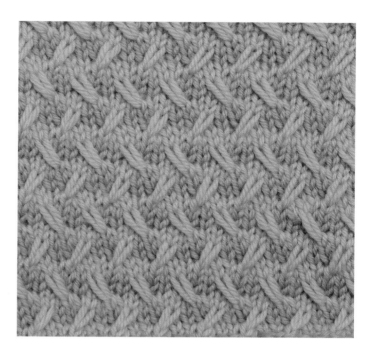

Front

Special abbreviations

c3L: cable three left
Slip the next stitch on to a cable needle and hold it at the front of the work, knit the next two stitches from the left-hand needle, then knit the stitch from the cable needle.

c3R: cable three right
Slip the next two stitches on to the cable needle and hold this at the back of the work, knit the next stitch from the left-hand needle, then knit the stitches from the cable needle.

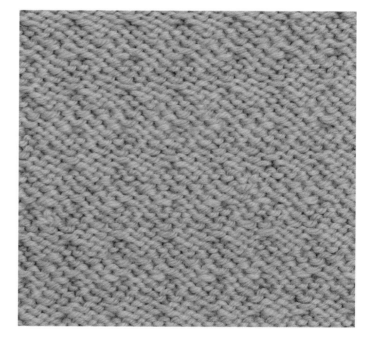

Back

TIP You could knit this stitch using one colour instead of two, to produce a textured stitch without the contrasting stripes.

Rice Stitch

This dainty two-colour stitch resembles grains of rice. Like many colourwork stitches, the wrong side is untidy and should be hidden in finished items.

To work rice stitch:

Use yarn in two colours, A and B.

Cast on an even number of stitches, using yarn A.
Row 1 (RS): using A, *sl1, k1; rep from * to end.
Row 2: using A, purl.
Row 3: using B, *k1, sl1; rep from * to end.
Row 4: using B, purl.

Rows 1–4 form the pattern; repeat these rows until the work is the desired length.

Houndstooth

This stitch creates a firm fabric, and is best suited to structured knits such as tailored jackets and bags and belts.

To work houndstooth:

Use yarn in two colours, A and B.

Cast on a multiple of three stitches, using yarn A.
Row 1 (RS): using yarn A, k1, *sl1 purlwise, k2; rep from * to last 2 sts, sl1 purlwise, k1.
Row 2: using yarn A, purl.
Row 3: using yarn B, *sl1 purlwise, k2; rep from * to end.
Row 4: using yarn B, purl.

Rows 1–4 form the pattern; repeat these rows until the work is the desired length.

TIP Slip all stitches purlwise to avoid twisting them.

Necklace Stitch

These wavy stripes resemble rows of beads. Choose four harmonising colours for a pretty effect or four contrasting colours for more definition. The fabric is firm and thick, with loops of yarn stranded across the reverse and up the side, so bear this in mind when choosing your project.

To work necklace stitch:

Use yarn in four colours, A, B, C and D.

Cast on a multiple of six stitches, plus two, using yarn A.

Row 1 (RS): using A, k2, *sl4, k2; rep from * to end.
Row 2: using A, k1, p2, *sl2, p4; rep from * to last 5 sts, sl2, p2, k1.
Row 3: using A, knit.
Row 4: using A, k1, p to last st, k1.
Row 5: using B, k1, sl2; *k2, sl4; rep from * to last 5 sts, k2, sl2, k1.
Row 6: using B, k1, yfwd, sl1, *p4, sl2; rep from * to last 6 sts, p4, sl1, k1.
Row 7: using B, knit.
Row 8: using B, k1, p to last st, k1.
Row 9: using C, k2, *sl4, k2; rep from * to end.
Row 10: using C, k1, p2, *sl2, p4; rep from * to last 5 sts, sl2, p2, k1.
Row 11: using C, knit.
Row 12: using C, k1, p to last st, k1.
Row 13: using D, k1, sl2, *k2, sl4; rep from * to last 5 sts, k2, sl2, k1.
Row 14: using D, k1, yfwd, sl1, *p4, sl2; rep from * to last 6 sts, p4, sl1, k1.
Row 15: using D, knit.
Row 16: using D, k1, p to last st, k1.

Rows 1–16 form the pattern; repeat these rows until the work is the desired length.

Front

Back

Note: slip all slip stitches purlwise.

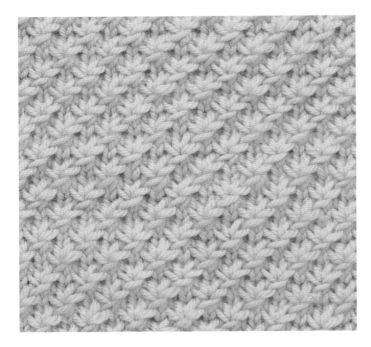

Front

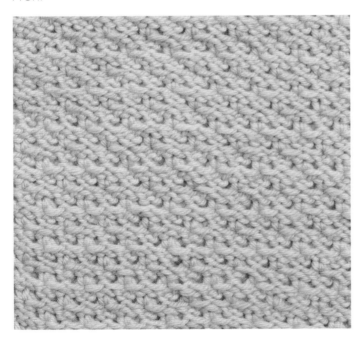

Back

Star Stitch

This two-colour stitch pattern creates both colour and texture, with raised stars forming attractive stripes. The thickness of the fabric makes it ideal for a mug hug or a coffee pot or teapot cover. You could also use it for accessories or garments where a thick fabric without too much stretch would be an advantage.

To work star stitch:

Use yarn in two colours, A and B.

Cast on a multiple of four stitches, plus one, using yarn A.
Row 1 (RS): using A, knit.
Row 2: using A, p1, *MS, p1; rep from * to end.
Row 3: using B, knit.
Row 4: p3, *MS, p1; rep from * to last 2 sts, p2.

Rows 1–4 form the pattern; repeat these rows until the work is the desired length.

Special abbreviations

MS: make star
Purl the next three stitches together (p3tog), leaving these stitches on the left-hand needle, wrap the yarn around the needle, then purl the same three stitches together again, this time transferring the stitch on to the right-hand needle.

TIP By purling three stitches together, you reduce three stitches to just one, but by taking the yarn around the needle, you create an additional stitch, then by purling the same three stitches together again, you create a third stitch, so you make a textured 'star' but the stitch count remains the same.

Hurdle Stitch

This small-scale brick pattern is worked on two double-pointed needles. Dropped stitches form neat upright strands, breaking up rows of garter stitches into little blocks. The sides and back of the work are tidy and the fabric lies reasonably flat, making it quite versatile.

To work hurdle stitch:

Use yarn in two colours, A and B.

Cast on a multiple of four stitches, plus three, using two double-pointed needles and yarn A.

Row 1 (RS): using A, *k3, yfwd, k1; rep from * to last 3 sts, k3; do not turn but push sts to other end of needle.

Row 2: with RS facing, using B, *k3, drop loop, sl1; rep from * to last 3 sts, k3; turn.

Row 3: using B, *k3, yfwd, sl1, yb; rep from * to last 3 sts, k3; do not turn but push sts to other end of needle.

Row 4 (WS): using A, p2, *yrn, p4; rep from * to last st, yrn, p1; turn.

Row 5: using B, k1, *drop loop, sl1, k3; rep from * to last 3 sts, drop loop, sl1, k1; turn.

Row 6: using B, k1, *yfwd, sl1, yb, k3; rep from * to last 2 sts, yfwd, sl1, yb, k1; turn.

Rows 1–6 form the pattern; repeat these rows until the work is the desired length.

Front

Back

TIP The instruction 'drop loop' is to drop the stitch formed by the 'yfwd' or 'yrn' on the previous row.

Front

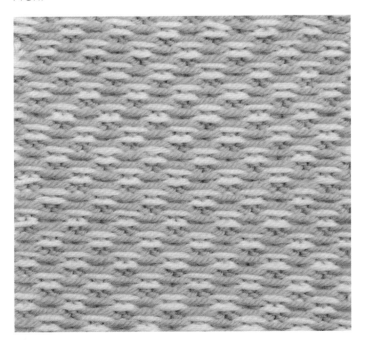

Back

TIP **You will be using two different yarns in each row. On right-side rows, carry the yarn not in use loosely across the back of the work. On wrong-side rows, carry the yarn not in use across the front of the work. This will create strands of yarn on the wrong side of the work.**

Check Stitch

This chequerboard pattern, which uses the Fair Isle knitting technique, has a definite right and wrong side. The wrong side, which has horizontal loops of yarn across every row, should always be hidden, so use this stitch for garments such as sweaters, where the wrong side will not be on show, for accessories such as hats or socks, or for homewares such as cushion covers or hot water bottle covers.

To work check stitch:

Use yarn in two colours, A and B.

Cast on a multiple of four stitches, using yarn A.
Row 1 (RS): k3A, *k2B, k2A; rep from * to last st, k1A.
Row 2: p3A, *p2B, p2A; rep from * to last st, p1A.
Row 3: k1A, *k2B, k2A; rep from * to last 3 sts, k2B, k1A.
Row 4: p1A, *p2B, p2A; rep from * to last 3 sts, p2B, p1A.

Rows 1–4 form the pattern; repeat these rows until the work is the desired length.

Three-colour Check Stitch

This neat checked design would be lovely as an allover fabric for a tea cosy, with the added advantage of the thickness of the fabric that will add a thermal dimension. For the same reason, it would be a good choice for a warm hat, mittens, muff or cowl.

To work three-colour check stitch:

Use yarn in three colours, A, B and C.

Cast on a multiple of four stitches, using yarn A.
Row 1 (WS): using A, purl.
Row 2: using B, k3, sl2, *k2, sl2; rep from * to last 3 sts, k3.
Row 3: using B, p3, sl2, *p2, sl2; rep from * to last 3 sts, p3.
Row 4: using A, knit.
Row 5: using C, p1, sl2, *p2, sl2; rep from * to last st, p1.
Row 6: using C, k1, sl2, *k2, sl2; rep from * to last st, k1.

Rows 1–6 form the pattern; repeat these rows until the work is the desired length.

TIP Yarns not in use should be carried up each side of the work. When doing this, be sure to keep the strands fairly loose. These strands will be hidden in the seams when joining pieces together.

Front

Back

Note: slip all slip stitches purlwise.

Front

Back

TIP Like many other colourwork stitches, only one colour is used on each pair of rows, the yarns not in use being carried up the side of the work. When doing this, try to keep the strands fairly loose.

Tweed Stitch

Forming a three-colour garter stitch fabric with a tweedy, flecked pattern, this stitch has a definite right side – but on the wrong side, the yarn strands are short and neat, so this stitch could be used for cardigans, jackets and other garments where the wrong side might be glimpsed. The right-hand edge however, is a little untidy, where yarns not in use are carried up the side, so this is best hidden. The fabric lies quite flat, so there is no need for blocking.

To work tweed stitch:

Use yarn in three colours, A, B and C.

Cast on a multiple of four stitches plus three, using yarn A.

Row 1 (RS): using B, k1, *sl1, k3; rep from * to last 2 sts, sl1, k1.

Row 2: using B, k1, *yfwd, sl1, yb, k3; rep from * to last 2 sts, yfwd, k1.

Row 3: using C, k3, *sl1, k3; rep from * to end.

Row 4: using C, k3, *yfwd, sl1, yb, k3; rep from * to end.

Row 5: using A, k1, *sl1, k3; rep from * to last 2 sts, sl1, k1.

Row 6: using A, k1, *yfwd, sl1, yb, k3; rep from * to last 2 sts, yfwd, sl1, yb, k1.

Row 7: using B, k3, * sl1, k3; rep from * to end.

Row 8: using B, k3, *yfwd, sl1, yb, k3; rep from * to end.

Row 9: using yarn C, k1, *sl1, k3; rep from * to last 2 sts, sl1, k1.

Row 10: using C, k1, *yfwd, sl1, yb, k3; rep from * to last 2 sts, yfd, sl1, yb, k1.

Row 11: using A, k3, *sl1, k3; rep from * to end.

Row 12: using A, k3, *yfwd, sl1, yb, k3; rep from * to end.

Rows 1–12 form the pattern; repeat these rows until the work is the desired length.

Brick Stitch

If you require a brickwork effect for toys or novelty knits, this stitch is ideal. It is deceptively simple to work because, like many colourwork stitches, though it features two colours, only one is in use at any one time, the pattern being cleverly created by strategically placed slip stitches. The finished fabric lies quite flat and does not require blocking.

To work brick stitch:

Use yarn in two colours, A and B.

Cast on a multiple of six stitches plus three, using yarn A.

Row 1 (RS): using A, knit.

Row 2: using A, purl.

Row 3: using B, k4, sl1, *k5, sl1; rep from * to last 4 sts, k4.

Row 4: using B, k4, yfwd, sl1, yb; rep from * to last 4 sts, k4.

Row 5: using B, p4, yb, sl1, yfwd, *p5, yb, sl1, yfwd; rep from * to last 4 sts, p4.

Row 6: as row 4.

Row 7: using A, knit.

Row 8: using A, purl.

Row 9: using B, k1, sl1, *k5, sl1; rep from * to last st, k1.

Row 10: using B, k1, yfwd, sl1, yb, *k5, yfwd, sl1, yb; rep from * to last st, k1.

Row 11: using B, p1, yb, sl1, yfwd, *p5, yb, sl1, yfwd; rep from * to last st, p1.

Row 12: as row 10.

Rows 1–12 form the pattern; repeat these rows until the work is the desired length.

Front

Back

TIP **Carry the yarn not in use up the side of the work, trying to keep the strands fairly loose.**

Front

Weaver Stitch

This double-sided fabric is attractive, easy to work, and has many practical applications. The back is not the same as the front but it is very neat, and so are the side edges; the fabric is firm and lies flat. Use it to make table mats, coasters, curtain tie-backs, rugs and other similar items.

To work weaver stitch:

Use yarn in two colours, A and B.

Cast on an even number of stitches, using yarn A.
Row 1 (RS): using A, *k1, yfwd, sl1, yb; rep from * to end.
Row 2: using A, *p1, yb, sl1, yfwd; rep from * to end.
Row 3: using B, *k1, yfwd, sl1, yb; rep from * to end.
Row 4 using B, *p1, yb, sl1, yfwd; rep from * to end.

Rows 1–4 form the pattern; repeat these rows until the work is the desired length.

Back

Note: slip all slip stitches purlwise.

Tapestry Stitch

Using two contrasting colours, this stitch resembles canvaswork or tapestry stitches and forms a thickly textured striped fabric. The stripes are subtle when the colours harmonise with each other and are more apparent if the contrast is stronger.

To work tapestry stitch:

Use yarn in two colours, A and B.

Cast on an uneven number of stitches, using yarn A.

Row 1 (RS): using A, *sl1, yrn, psso, k1; rep from * to end.

Row 2: using A, purl.

Row 3: using B, k1, sl1, yrn, psso; rep from * to end.

Row 4: using B, purl.

Rows 1–4 form the pattern; repeat these rows until the work is the desired length.

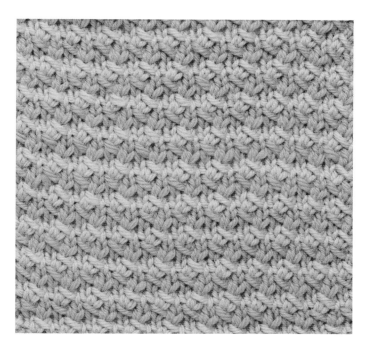

Front

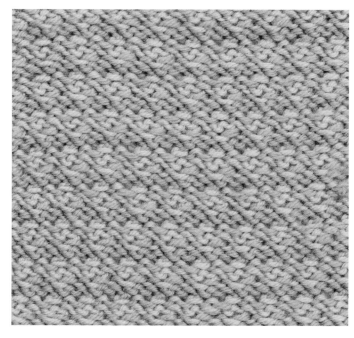

Back

TIP Though this is not a difficult stitch, it requires a bit of dexterity. In the first and third pattern rows, you will need to slip the first stitch, knit the next stitch, then take the yarn around the needle. You then pass the slipped stitch over both the knit stitch and the loop produced by bringing the yarn around the needle. This is easier after the first two rows have been completed, as the slipped stitches will be a different colour and therefore easier to identify.

Note: slip all slip stitches purlwise.

Front

Lattice Stitch

This two-colour novelty stitch creates an interesting design and a firm fabric, the name referring not so much to the colour pattern but the texture of the fabric. The reverse is neat, making it suitable for many applications such as bags, jackets, waistcoats and various home makes.

To work lattice stitch:

Use yarn in two colours, A and B.

Cast on a multiple of six stitches plus five, using yarn A.

Row 1 (RS): using A, knit.
Row 2: using A, purl.
Row 3: using B, k4, *yfwd, sl3, yb, k3; rep from * to last st, k1.
Row 4: using B, p4, *yb, sl3, yfwd, p3; rep from * to last st, p1.
Row 5: using A, knit.
Row 6: using A, purl.
Row 7: using A, k5, *pull loop and k1, k5; rep from * to end.
Row 8: using A, purl.
Row 9: using B, k1, *yfwd, sl3, yb, k3; rep from * to last 4 sts, yfwd, sl3, yb, k1.
Row 10: using B, p1, *yb, sl3, yfwd, p3; rep from * to last 4 sts, yb, sl3, yfwd, p1.
Row 11: using A, knit.
Row 12: using A, purl.
Row 13: using A, k2, *pull loop and k1, k5; rep from * to last 3 sts, pull loop and k1, k2.
Row 14: using A, purl.

Rows 3–14 form the pattern; repeat these rows until the work is the desired length.

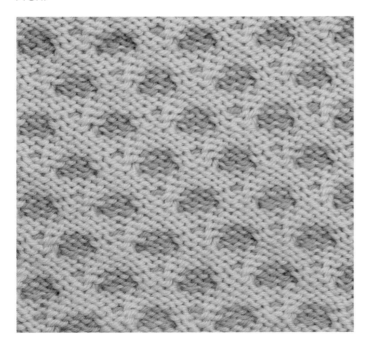

Back

Note: slip all slip stitches purlwise, and see opposite page for special abbreviations.

TIP **Take care to maintain an even tension, especially when stranding yarn across the front of the work.**

Step Stitch

This cute step pattern is cleverly constructed with strategically placed slip stitches and is easy to do. The thick fabric has a definite right and wrong side. It would be suitable for cushion covers or other items where the reverse would not be visible, so bear this in mind when considering this stitch.

To work step stitch:

Use yarn in two colours, A and B.

Cast on a multiple of four stitches, using yarn A.
Row 1 (WS): using A, purl.
Row 2: using B, *sl1, k3; rep from * to end.
Row 3: using B, *sl1, k3; rep from * to end.
Row 4: using A, *k1, sl1, k2; rep from * to end.
Row 5: using A, *p2, sl1, k2; rep from * to end.
Row 6: using B, *k2, sl1, k1; rep from * to end.
Row 7: using B, *p1, sl1, p2; rep from * to end.
Row 8: using A, *k3, sl1; rep from * to end.
Row 9: using A, *sl1, p3; rep from * to end.

Rows 2–9 form the pattern; repeat these rows until the work is the desired length.

Special abbreviations

pull loop and k1
Insert the point of the right-hand needle under the two strands of yarn B below, from the top, pull up and over the left-hand needle and behind the first stitch. Knit the first stitch and at the same time drop the two strands of yarn B to the back of the work.

Front

Back

Note: slip all slip stitches purlwise.

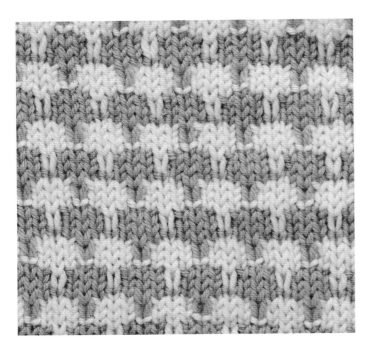

Front

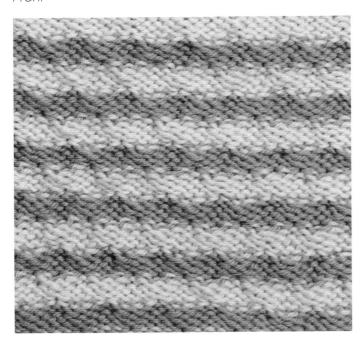

Back

Fuchsia Stitch

Once you understand the technique of lifting up loops of yarn, this is a deceptively easy stitch and relatively quick to work, creating an attractive variation of stocking stitch stripes. With a neat wrong side, it can be used for all kinds of garments and accessories, including hats.

To work fuchsia stitch:

Use yarn in two colours, A and B.

Cast on a multiple of four stitches plus three, using yarn A.

Row 1 (RS): using A, knit.
Row 2: using A, purl.
Row 3: using B, knit.
Row 4: using B, purl.
Row 5: as row 3.
Row 6: as row 4.
Row 7: using A, *k3, pick up loop, k1 and pass loop over; rep from * to last 3 sts, k3.
Row 8: using A, purl.
Row 9: using A, knit.
Row 10: as row 8.
Row 11: using B, k1, *pick up loop, k1 and pass loop over, k3; rep from * to last 2 sts, pick up loop, k1 and pass loop over, k1.
Row 12: using B, purl.

Rows 5–12 form the pattern; repeat these rows until the work is the desired length.

Special abbreviations

pick up loop, k1 and pass loop over
Before knitting the next stitch, pick up a loop of the same colour from the corresponding stitch four rows below. Keeping that loop on the right-hand needle, knit the next stitch in the current row then pass the loop over this stitch and off the needle.

Reversible Stocking Stitch

This clever stitch produces a thick double-sided fabric that has lots of practical uses. Having neat edges on all four sides, it would make a cosy coverlet for a pram or crib, or perhaps a bedside rug. Knitted in a cotton yarn, it would make a practical bath mat or, on a smaller scale, a pot holder, teapot stand or coaster. It is knitted using two double-pointed needles.

To work reversible stocking stitch:

Use yarn in two colours, A and B.

Cast on an even number of stitches, using two double-pointed needles and yarn A.

Row 1: using A, *k1, yfwd, sl1, yb; rep from * to end; do not turn but push sts to other end of needle.

Row 2: using B, *yb, sl1, yfwd, p1; rep from * to end; turn.

Row 3: using B, *k1, yfwd, sl1, yb; rep from * to end; do not turn but push sts to other end of needle.

Row 4: using A, *yb, sl1, yfwd, p1; rep from * to end; turn.

Rows 1–4 form the pattern; repeat these rows until the work is the desired length.

Front

Back

TIP At the ends of rows 2 and 4, when you turn the work, make sure the yarns are crossed over each other to create neat selvedges.

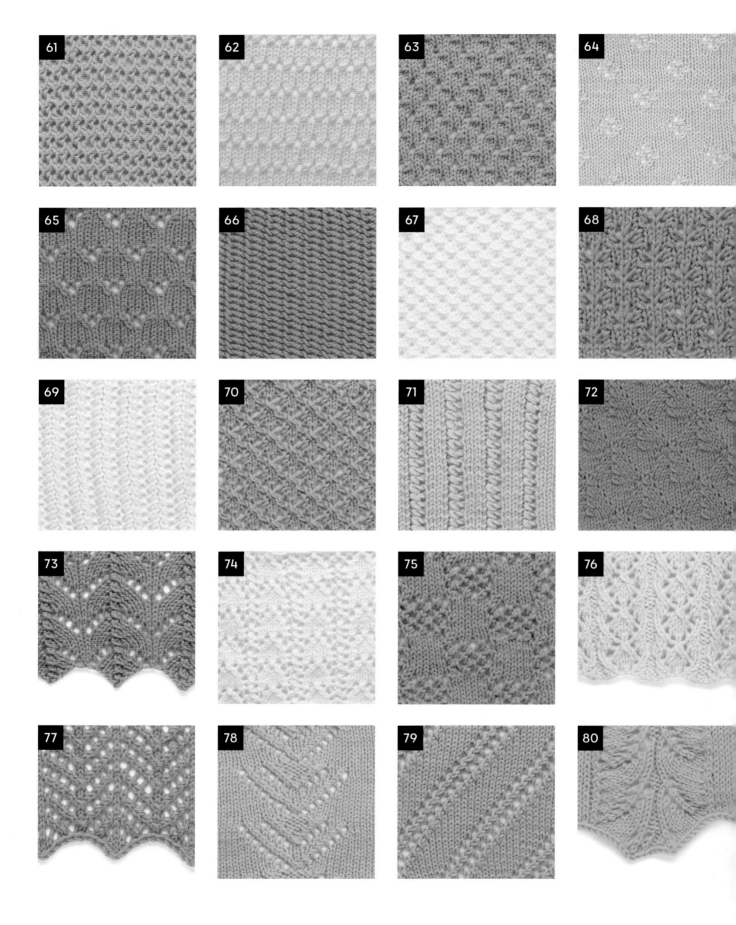

Lacy Stitches

Openwork

This is the ideal stitch for making cellular blankets. It works well with yarns made from various fibres, but especially cotton. It can also be used for summer tops and scarves, among other things. The fabric is double-sided, so is well suited for scarves and shawls too. It is easy to do and the work grows relatively quickly, making it ideal for larger projects.

To work openwork:

Cast on an uneven number of stitches.
Row 1: k1, *yfwd, k2tog; rep from * to end.
Row 2: purl.
Row 3: *skpo, yfwd; rep from * to last st, k1.
Row 4: purl.

Rows 1–4 form the pattern; repeat these rows until the work is the desired length.

Front

Back

TIP You can find a list of abbreviations on page 24. This includes the 'skpo' used in this pattern, where you slip the next stitch purlwise, knit the next stitch, then pass the slipped stitch over the knitted stitch and off the needle. This reduces the stitch count by one, but it is followed by a 'yfwd' – yarn forward – which adds a stitch, thereby replacing the decreased stitch and restoring the stitch count to what it was before.

Eyelet Rows

Here, evenly spaced eyelets form neat rows on a background of stocking stitch. This is an easy stitch that grows quickly. It has an obvious right and wrong side and has a tendency to curl, so will need blocking.

To work eyelet rows:

Cast on an even number of stitches.
Row 1 (RS): knit.
Row 2: purl.
Row 3: knit.
Row 4: purl.
Row 5: k1, *k2tog, yfwd; rep from * to last st, k1.
Row 6: purl.

Rows 1–6 form the pattern; repeat these rows until the work is the desired length.

Alternating Eyelets

This stitch, a stocking stitch fabric with a regular pattern made up of staggered rows of eyelet holes, can be substituted in almost any pattern that uses stocking stitch. It is ideal for sweaters, cardigans and summer tops as well as for baby clothes. It can be used as an allover stitch or in panels, and combines well with other stitches. It will benefit from being blocked as it has a tendency to curl.

To work alternating eyelets:

Cast on a multiple of four stitches plus three.
Row 1 (RS): knit.
Row 2: purl.
Row 3: *k2, k2tog, yfwd; rep from * to last 3 sts, k3.
Row 4: purl.
Row 5: knit.
Row 6: purl.
Row 7: *k2tog, yfwd, k2; rep from * to last 3 sts, k2tog, yfwd, k1.
Row 8: purl.

Rows 1–8 form the pattern; repeat these rows until the work is the desired length.

Diamond Eyelets

This stitch features alternating rows of diamonds composed of four eyelet holes against a background of stocking stitch. Like some of the other plainer lacy stitches, this stitch pattern can be substituted in almost any pattern that uses stocking stitch and is ideal for garments such as sweaters, cardigans and summer tops, baby clothes and accessories. It can be combined with other stitches. As with other stocking stitch fabrics, it has a tendency to curl, so will benefit from blocking.

To work diamond eyelets:

Cast on a multiple of 12 stitches plus seven.

Row 1 (RS): *k2, k2tog, yfwd, k8; rep from * to last 7 sts, k2, k2tog, yfwd, k3.

Row 2: purl.

Row 3: *k1, k2tog, yfwd, k2tog, yfwd, k7; rep from * to last 7 sts, k1, k2tog, yfwd, k2tog, yfwd, k2.

Row 4: purl.

Row 5: as row 1.

Row 6: purl.

Row 7: knit.

Row 8: purl.

Row 9: *k8, k2tog, yfwd, k2; rep from * to last 7 sts, k7.

Row 10: purl.

Row 11: *k7, k2tog, yfwd, k2tog, yfwd, k1; rep from * to last 7 sts, k7.

Row 12: purl.

Row 13: as row 9.

Row 14: purl.

Row 15: knit.

Row 16: purl.

Rows 1–16 form the pattern; repeat these rows until the work is the desired length.

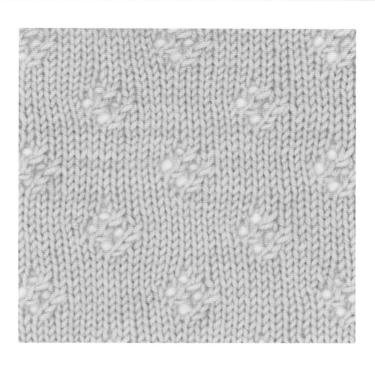

Front

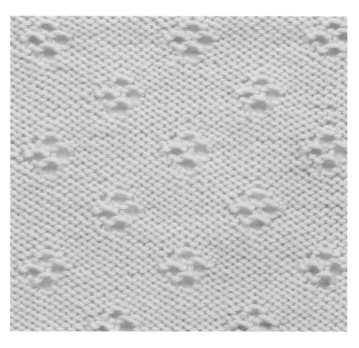

Back

TIP Ideally, choose a smooth yarn that gives good stitch definition for this and for most other lacy stitches in order to show off the stitch pattern well. Using a fuzzy yarn will tend to make the stitch pattern less distinct.

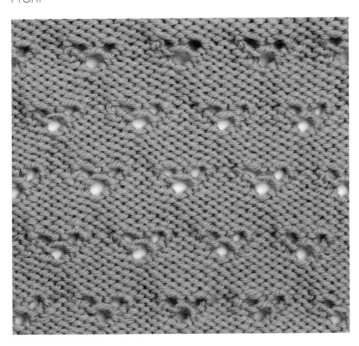

Front

Back

Little Flowers

This is a simple and versatile lacy stitch with a stocking stitch background. Groups of three eyelets, arranged in rows to create a regular pattern, make an ideal fabric for all kinds of garments, baby clothes and accessories. This stitch is quick and easy to do and can be used in place of plain stocking stitch.

To work little flowers:

Cast on a multiple of six stitches plus three.
Row 1 (RS): knit.
Row 2: purl.
Row 3: knit.
Row 4: purl.
Row 5: *k4, yfwd, skpo; rep from * to last 3 sts, k3.
Row 6: purl.
Row 7: k1, *k1, k2tog, yfwd, k1, yfwd, skpo; rep from * to last 2 sts, k2.
Row 8: purl.
Row 9: knit.
Row 10: purl.
Row 11: knit.
Row 12: purl.
Row 13: k1, yfwd, skpo, *k4, yfwd, skpo; rep from * to end.
Row 14: purl.
Row 15: *k1, yfwd, skpo, k1, k2tog, yfwd; rep from * to last 2 sts, k2.
Row 16: purl.

Rows 1–16 form the pattern; repeat these rows until the work is the desired length.

TIP This pattern may appear complicated, with a 16-row pattern repeat, but you will see on closer inspection that all but four of the rows are simply knit or purl, making it relatively simple.

Faggoting

This stitch pattern produces a cellular fabric with slightly larger holes that is ideal for summer tops and dresses as well as for blankets and throws.

To work faggoting:

Cast on an even number of stitches.

Row 1 (RS): k1, *yrn, p2tog; rep from * to last st, k1.

Row 1 forms the pattern; repeat this row until the work is the desired length.

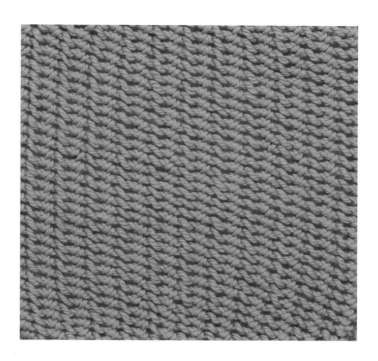

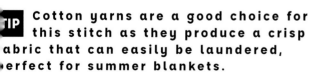 **Cotton yarns are a good choice for this stitch as they produce a crisp fabric that can easily be laundered, perfect for summer blankets.**

Knotted Openwork

This is a very easy stitch that grows quickly to produce a fabric with a thick, springy texture. There is a definite right and wrong side, but both sides are attractive, making this stitch pattern excellent for throws and blankets as well as clothes, accessories such as scarves and shawls, and homewares.

To work knotted openwork:

Cast on an even number of stitches.
Row 1 (WS): purl.
Row 2: k2, *yfwd, MK; rep from * to last st, k1.
Row 3: purl.
Row 4: k1, *MK, yfwd; rep from * to last 2 sts, k2.
Row 5: purl.

Rows 2–5 form the pattern; repeat these rows until the work is the desired length.

Special abbreviations

MK = make knot
Knit three stitches then, with the left-hand needle, lift the first of these stitches over the other two and off the needle.

Butterfly Lace

As lace stitches go, this one has a pretty pattern but a fairly close fabric – not too open and airy – so it is a good choice for all-seasons garments for all ages. It would look particularly effective as a panel in an otherwise plain stocking stitch fabric. It could also be used for homewares, such as cushion covers.

To work butterfly lace:

Cast on a multiple of eight stitches plus seven.

Row 1 (RS): k1, *k2tog, yfwd, k1, yfwd, skpo, k3; rep from * ending last rep k1 instead of k3.

Row 2: p3, *sl1, p7; rep from * to last 4 sts, sl1, p3.

Row 3: as row 1.

Row 4: as row 2.

Row 5: k5, *k2tog, yfwd, k1, yfwd, skpo, k3; rep from * to last 2 sts, k2.

Row 6: p7, *sl1, p7; rep from * to end.

Row 7: as row 5.

Row 8: as row 6.

Rows 1–8 form the pattern; repeat these rows until the work is the desired length.

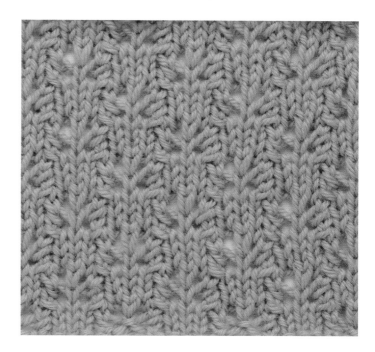

Front

Back

TIP If you were to use this stitch to create a cushion cover, it would be a good idea to first cover the cushion pad in a plain-coloured fabric that contrasts with the colour of the yarn, as the fabric can be glimpsed through the holes in the knitted cover. This applies to other lacy stitches too, of course.

Note: slip all slip stitches purlwise.

Front

Back

Ridged Lace

This openwork rib stitch has the appearance of ribbing but not the stretch. It makes a good allover stitch for garments where you desire a textured fabric and ribbed appearance, such as a chunky winter sweater, and is also good for accessories such as hats and scarves. It would make a nice pram cover, too.

To work ridged lace:

Cast on a multiple of four stitches plus two.
Row 1 (RS): k3, *yfwd, skpo, k2; rep from * to last 3 sts, yfwd, skpo, k1.
Row 2: p3, *yrn, p2tog, p2; rep from * to last 3 sts, yrn, p2tog, p1.

Rows 1 and 2 form the pattern; repeat these rows until the work is the desired length.

Special abbreviations

yfwd = yarn forward
Bring the yarn from the back to the front of the work, between the two needles, before working the next instruction. This creates a new stitch.

yrn = yarn round needle
Take the yarn around the right-hand needle to form a loop that will become a new stitch. In this pattern, when working a 'yrn' in row 2 of the pattern, the yarn will begin and end at the front of the work.

Diamond Lace

This lovely lace pattern is not difficult to do, with only four pattern rows on which to concentrate. Though there is a definite right and wrong side, this stitch is suitable not only for jumpers, where the wrong side would not show, but also for cardigans, scarves, shawls and blankets.

To work diamond lace:

Cast on a multiple of six stitches plus one.

Row 1 (RS): *k1, k2tog, yfwd, k1, yfwd, k2tog tbl; rep from * to last st, k1.

Row 2: purl.

Row 3: k2tog, *yfwd, k3, yfwd, (sl1) twice, k1, p2sso; rep from * to last 5 sts, yfwd, k3, yfwd, k2tog tbl.

Row 4: purl.

Row 5: *k1, yfwd, k2tog tbl, k1, k2tog, yfwd; rep from * to last st, k1.

Row 6: purl.

Row 7: k2, *yfwd, (sl1) twice, k1, p2sso, yfwd, k3; rep from * to last 5 sts, yfwd, (sl1) twice, k1, p2sso, yfwd, k2.

Row 8: purl.

Rows 1–8 form the pattern; repeat these rows until the work is the desired length.

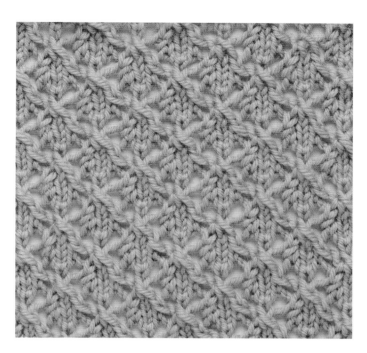

Front

Special abbreviations

(sl1) twice
Slip the next two stitches, one at a time, from the left-hand to the right-hand needle. Be sure to slip each stitch purlwise – in other words, passing the tip of the needle from right to left under the stitch loop, as if you were going to make a purl stitch – to avoid the stitch loops becoming twisted.

p2sso
Pass the two slip stitches over the stitch you just knitted.

Back

TIP Some instructions ask you to knit two stitches together (k2tog) and some to knit two stitches together through the back loops (k2tog tbl). Each causes the stitch loops to lean in different directions. This is essential for creating the distinctive stitch pattern.

Front

Back

Ladder Lace

With its vertical rows of neat eyelets, this lace pattern would be a good choice for a flattering sweater in a cotton yarn for summer or something warmer for winter. Though the two sides of the fabric look different – the right side with vertical bands of stocking stitch and the wrong side with the same bands in reverse stocking stitch – you could use this for blankets and throws as well as for garments and accessories. The finished work should be blocked in order to flatten the fabric and open up the pattern.

To work ladder lace:

Cast on a multiple of six stitches plus three.
Row 1 (RS): k3, *yrn, sl1k, k2tog, psso, yrn, k3; rep from * to end.
Row 2: purl.

Rows 1 and 2 form the pattern; repeat these rows until the work is the desired length.

Special abbreviations

sl1k = slip one knitwise
Slip the stitch knitwise. This means you should insert the right-hand needle into the next stitch as if you were going to knit it but, instead of knitting it, you simply slip it from the left-hand to the right-hand needle.

TIP Though there are only two rows to this pattern, the way you have to manipulate the stitches and create new stitches by winding the yarn around the right-hand needle can make it a little tricky to work if you are an inexperienced knitter. Practice makes perfect!

Falling Leaves

Once you have mastered the simpler lacy patterns, you might want to try something a little more challenging. This classic lace pattern requires a little more concentration but the results are worth it, especially if you are a fan of vintage fashion. This would be a good choice for a fitted top or a fit-and-flare jumper, a cardigan, or lacy baby clothes with an old-fashioned, heirloom quality.

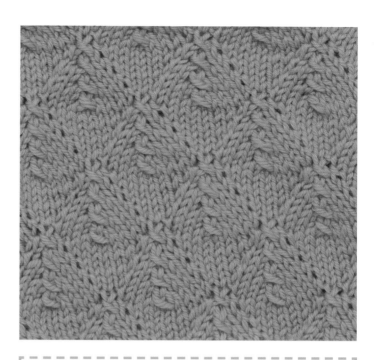

To work falling leaves:

Cast on a multiple of ten stitches plus six.

Row 1 (RS): k1, yrn, *k3, sl1, k2tog, psso, k3, M1, k1, M1; rep from * to last 5 sts, k3, skpo.

Row 2: purl.

Row 3: k2, M1, *k2, sl1, k2tog, psso, k2, M1, k3, M1; rep from * to last 4 sts, k2, skpo.

Row 4: purl.

Row 5: k3, M1, *k1, sl1, k2tog, psso, k1, M1, k5, M1; rep from * to last 3 sts, k1, skpo.

Row 6: purl.

Row 7: k4, M1, *sl1, k2tog, psso, M1, k7, M1; rep from * to last 2 sts, skpo.

Row 8: purl.

Row 9: skpo, k3, M1, *k1, M1, k3, sl1, k2tog, psso, k3, M1; rep from * to last st, k1.

Row 10: purl.

Row 11: skpo, k2, M1, k1, *k2, M1, k2, sl1, k2tog, psso, k2, M1, k1; rep from * to last st, k1.

Row 12: purl.

Row 13: skpo, k1, M1, k2, *k3, M1, k1, sl1, k2tog, psso, k1, M1, k2; rep from * to last st, k1.

Row 14: purl.

Row 15: skpo, M1, k3, *k4, M1, sl1, k2tog, psso, M1, k3; rep from * to last st, k1.

Row 16: purl.

Rows 1–16 form the pattern; repeat these rows until the work is the desired length.

Special abbreviations

sl1, k2tog, psso
You will come across this instruction in other patterns but it is worth having a reminder of how to do it. Slip the next stitch knitwise, knit the next two stitches together, then pass the slipped stitch over the stitch formed by the 'k2tog' and off the right-hand needle.

skpo
Slip the next stitch knitwise, knit the next stitch, then pass the slipped stitch over the knitted stitch and off the right-hand needle.

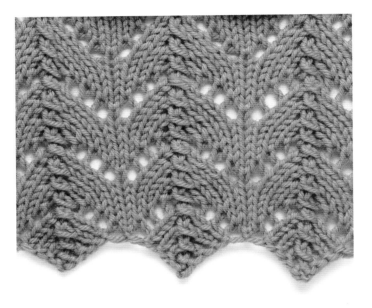

Front

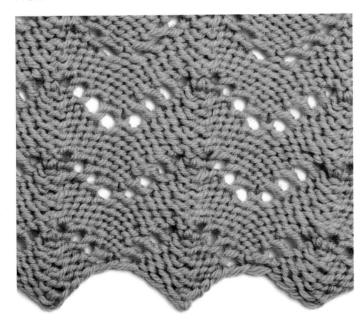

Back

Fishtail Lace

This lacy pattern, similar to Arrowhead Lace (see opposite) has a pattern that, resembles fishtails. Use it for garments, accessories, blankets and other items where you want a lacy look. The lower edge is beautifully scalloped, so make a feature of this on the hems of sweaters and the ends of scarves and shawls – or even on the rim of a hat.

To work fishtail lace:

Cast on a multiple of ten stitches plus one.
Row 1 (RS): k1, *yfwd, k3, sl1, k2tog, psso, k3, yfwd, k1; rep from * to end.
Row 2: purl.
Row 3: k2, *yfwd, k2, sl1, k2tog, psso, k2, yfwd, k3; rep from * ending last rep k2 instead of k3.
Row 4: purl.
Row 5: k3, *yfwd, k1, sl1, k2tog, psso, k1, yfwd, k5; rep from * ending last rep k3 instead of k5.
Row 6: purl.
Row 7: k4, *yfwd, sl1, k2tog, psso, yfwd, k7; rep from * ending last rep k4 instead of k7.
Row 8: purl.

Rows 1–8 form the pattern; repeat these rows until the work is the desired length.

TIP When following the instruction sl1, k2tog, psso, remember to slip the sli; stitch knitwise.

Arrowhead Lace

The distinctive pattern of upward-facing shapes resembles rows of arrowheads – hence the name of this classic allover lace stitch. Choose it for vintage-style sweaters, shrugs and other garments or for babywear. Though the two sides of the fabric look different, this stitch can also be used for blankets, shawls and other similar items.

To work arrowhead lace:

Cast on a multiple of eight stitches plus five.
Row 1 (WS): purl.
Row 2: k1, *yfwd, sl1, k2tog, psso, yfwd, k5; rep from * to last 4 sts, yfwd, sl1, k2tog, psso, yfwd, k1.
Row 3: purl.
Row 4: as row 2.
Row 5: purl.
Row 6: k4, *yfwd, skpo, k1, k2tog, yfwd, k3; rep from * to last st, k1.
Row 7: purl.
Row 8: k1, *yfwd, sl1, k2tog, psso, yfwd, k1; rep from * to end.
Row 9: purl.

Rows 2–9 form the pattern; repeat these rows until the work is the desired length.

Front

Back

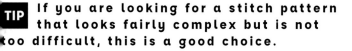

TIP If you are looking for a stitch pattern that looks fairly complex but is not too difficult, this is a good choice.

Chequerboard Lace

With a lovely pattern of stocking stitch and openwork squares, neatly arranged in alternating rows, use in place of plain stocking stitch if you want to add some pattern to a jumper or other garment. Bear in mind that the plain squares on the wrong side will be reverse stocking stitch.

Front

To work chequerboard lace:

Cast on a multiple of 12 stitches plus eight.
Row 1 (RS): k7, *(yfwd, k2tog) 3 times, k6; rep from * to last st, k1.
Row 2: purl.
Row 3: k7, *(k2tog, yfwd) 3 times, k6; rep from * to last st, k1.
Row 4: purl.
Row 5: as row 1.
Row 6: purl.
Row 7: as row 3.
Row 8: purl.
Row 9: k1, *(yfwd, k2tog) 3 times, k6; rep from * to last 7 sts, (yfwd, k2tog) 3 times, k1.
Row 10: purl.
Row 11: k1, *(k2tog, yfwd) 3 times, k6; rep from * to last 7 sts, (k2tog, yfwd) 3 times, k1.
Row 12: purl.
Row 13: as row 9.
Row 14: purl.
Row 15: as row 11.
Row 16: purl.

Rows 1–16 form the pattern; repeat these rows until the work is the desired length.

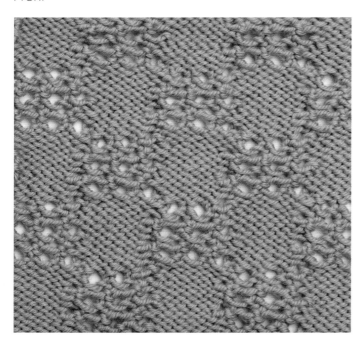

Back

TIP Novice knitters might need reminding that instructions in brackets need to be repeated. So the instruction '(yfwd, k2tog) 3 times' means that the stitch pattern inside the brackets needs to be repeated three times before moving on to the next instruction.

Diamond Rib Lace

Vertical columns of diamond eyelets form a pleasing pattern that would look good on all kinds of garments. Many lace stitches, such as this one, that have a shaped lower edge, can be used not only as an allover fabric but also as borders and hems. So you could work just one or two pattern repeats and then change to a plainer stitch.

To work diamond rib lace:

Cast on a multiple of nine stitches plus two.

Row 1 (RS): p2, *k2tog, (k1, yfwd) twice, k1, skpo, p2; rep from * to end.

Row 2: k2, *p7, k2; rep from * to end.

Row 3: p2, *k2tog, yfwd, k3, yfwd, skpo, p2; rep from * to end.

Row 4: as row 2.

Row 5: p2, *k1, yfwd, skpo, k1, k2tog, yfwd, k1, p2; rep from * to end.

Row 6: as row 2.

Row 7: p2, *k2, yfwd, sl1, k2tog, psso, yfwd, k2, p2; rep from * to end.

Row 8: as row 2.

Rows 1–8 form the pattern; repeat these rows until the work is the desired length.

Front

Back

TIP Many lace stitches have a shaped edge. This will be apparent when using it for something like a blanket or scarf where there is no border or ribbing, so bear this in mind if you are considering this stitch for your next project.

Front

Chevron Lace

This lacy stitch would be a good choice for a scarf or shawl: because of its construction, both the bottom (cast-on) and top (cast-off) edges are slightly wavy, which you could use as a feature. It would also make a lovely jumper or, of course, a blanket, throw or cushion cover.

To work chevron lace:

Cast on a multiple of ten stitches plus one.
Row 1 (RS): k1, *(yfwd, skpo) twice, k1, (k2tog, yfwd) twice, k1; rep from * to end.
Row 2: purl.
Row 3: k2, *yfwd, skpo, yfwd, sl1, k2tog, psso, yfwd, k2tog, yfwd, k3; rep from * to last 9 sts, yfwd, skpo, yfwd, sl1, k2tog, psso, yfwd, k2tog, yfwd, k2.
Row 4: purl.

Rows 1–4 form the pattern; repeat these rows until the work is the desired length.

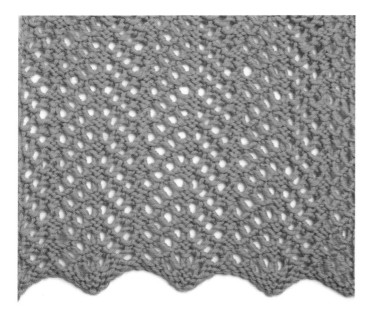

Back

TIP When blocking the finished pieces, pull the knitted fabric downwards slightly, to open out the holes in the lace and display it to good advantage.

Chevron Panel

This vertical strip of upward-facing chevrons is designed to be inserted as a panel on a ground of plain stocking stitch. It could be used on the front of a cardigan, with two panels, one on either side of the front opening; or you could place one or more of these panels on the front of a sweater. It has lots of potential applications.

To work chevron panel:

Cast on 17 stitches for the panel (plus an even number of extra stitches).

Row 1 (RS): (k1, yfwd, skpo) twice, p5, (k2tog, yfwd, k1) twice.
Row 2: p6, k5, p6.
Row 3: k2, yfwd, skpo, k1, yfwd, skpo, p3, k2tog, yfwd, k1, k2tog, yfwd, k2.
Row 4: p7, k3, p7.
Row 5: k3, yfwd, skpo, k1, yfwd, skpo, p1, k2tog, yfwd, k1, k2tog, yfwd, k3.
Row 6: p8, k1, p8.
Row 7: k4, yfwd, skpo, k1, yfwd, sl1, k2tog, psso, yfwd, k1, k2tog, yfwd, k4.
Row 8: purl.
Row 9: k5, yfwd, skpo, k3, k2tog, yfwd, k5.
Row 10: purl.
Row 11: k6, yfwd, skpo, k1, k2tog, yfwd, k6.
Row 12: purl.
Row 13: k7, yfwd, sl1, k2tog, psso, yfwd, k7.
Row 14: purl.

Rows 1–14 form the pattern; repeat these rows until the work is the desired length.

TIP Instructions are given for the panel only, which should be worked on a stocking stitch fabric. This means you need to add extra stitches on either side when casting on. When working the odd-numbered (right-side) rows, knit to the point where you wish the panel to begin, follow the instructions for the 17-stitch panel, then knit to the end of the row. On even-numbered rows, purl the stitches on either side of the panel.

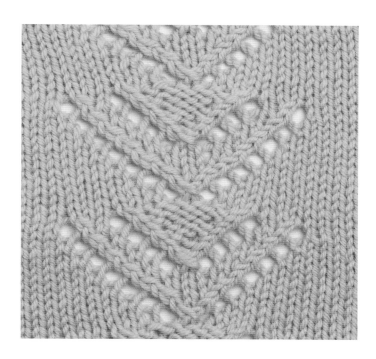

Front

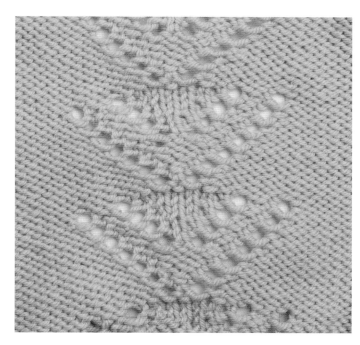

Back

Front

Back

Diagonal Lace

There are a lot of pattern rows involved in the construction of this stitch, but it is quite easy to knit. The diagonal 'dashes' form little lacy lines on an otherwise fairly solid fabric, making it a good choice for most garments and a suitable substitute for plain stocking stitch.

To work diagonal lace:

Cast on a multiple of seven stitches, plus one.
Row 1 (RS): k7, skpo, yfwd, k2tog, yfwd, *k6, skpo, yfwd, k2tog, yfwd; rep from * to last st, k1.
Row 2: purl.
Row 3: *k6, skpo, yfwd, k2tog, yfwd; rep from * to last 2 sts, k2.
Row 4: purl.
Row 5: k5, skpo, yfwd, k2tog, yfwd, *k6, skpo, yfwd, k2tog; rep from * to last 3 sts, k3.
Row 6: purl.
Row 7: k4, skpo, yfwd, k2tog, yfwd, *k6, skpo, yfwd, k2tog, yfwd; rep from * to last 4 sts, k4.
Row 8: purl.
Row 9: k3, skpo, yfwd, k2tog, yfwd, *k6, skpo, yfwd, k2tog, tfwd; rep from * to last 5 sts, k5.
Row 10: purl.
Row 11: k2, *skpo, yfwd, k2tog, yfwd, k6; rep from * to end.
Row 12: purl.
Row 13: k1, skpo, yfwd, k2tog, yfwd, *k6, skpo, yfwd, k2tog, yfwd; rep from * to last 7 sts, k7.
Row 14: purl.
Row 15: skpo, yfwd, k2tog, yfwd, *k6, skpo, yfwd, k2tog, yfwd; rep from * to last 8 sts, k8.
Row 16: purl.
Row 17: k1, *k2tog, yfwd, k6, skpo, yfwd; rep from * to last st, k1.
Row 18: purl.
Row 19: *k2tog, yfwd, k6, skpo, yfwd; rep from * to last 2 sts, k2.
Row 20: purl.

Rows 1–20 form the pattern; repeat these rows until the work is the desired length.

Leaf Panel Lace

Sometimes you want to create a feature, instead of using an allover stitch, and this classic lacy panel is an ideal starting point. It looks very effective in the middle of a stocking stitch fabric and is easier to work than you might think. It is also quicker to knit a jumper or other item that is mainly stocking stitch with just a hint of lace.

Front

To work leaf panel lace:

Cast on 24 stitches for the panel (plus an even number of extra stitches).

Row 1 (RS): sl1, k2tog, psso, k7, yfwd, k1, yrn, p2, yrn, k1, yfwd, k7, k3tog.
Row 2: p11, k2, p11.
Row 3: sl1, k2tog, psso, k6, (yfwd, k1) twice, p2, (k1, yfwd) twice, k6, k3tog.
Row 4: as row 2.
Row 5: sl1, k2tog, psso, k5, yfwd, k1, yfwd, k2, p2, k2, yfwd, k1, yfwd, k5, k3tog.
Row 6: as row 2.
Row 7: sl1, k2tog, psso, k4, yfwd, k1, yfwd, k4, p2, k4, yfwd, k1, yfwd, k3, k3tog.
Row 8: as row 2.
Row 9: sl1, k2tog, psso, k3, yfwd, k1, yfwd, k4, p2, k4, yfwd, k1, yfwd, k3, k2tog.
Row 10: as row 2.

Rows 1–10 form the pattern; repeat these rows until the work is the desired length.

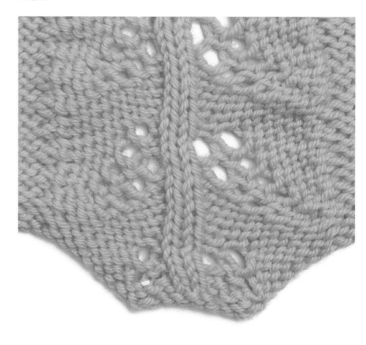

Back

TIP Instructions are given for the panel only. Depending on the extra number of stitches cast on, when working the odd-numbered (right-side) rows, knit to the beginning of the panel, follow the instructions for the 24-stitch panel, then knit to the end of the row. On even-numbered rows, purl the stitches on either side of the panel. This will produce a vertical leafy panel on a ground of plain stocking stitch.

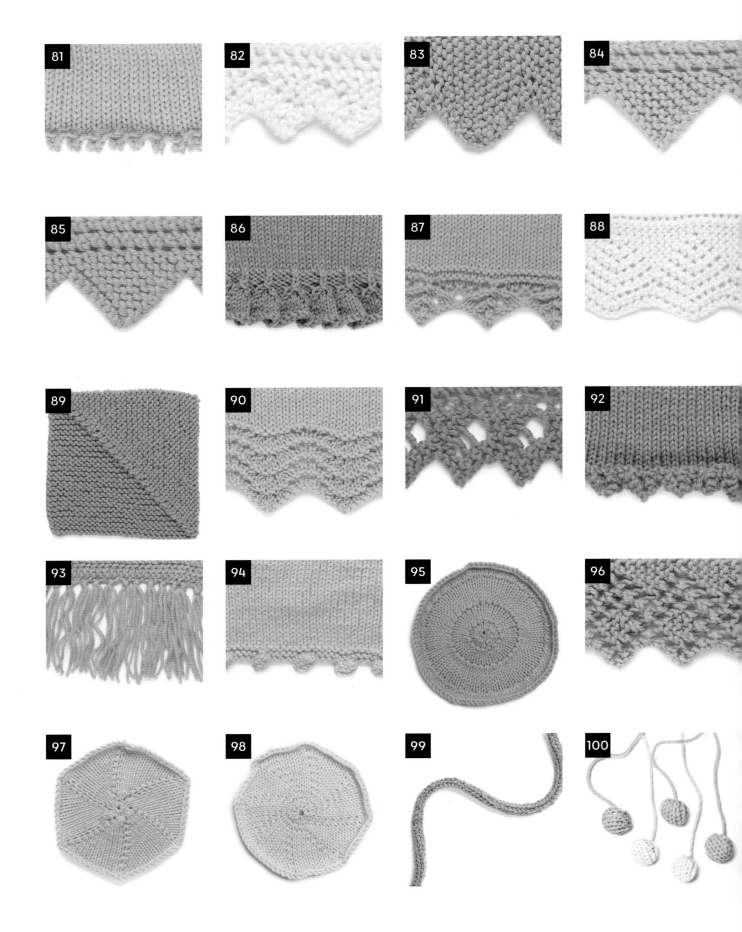

Finishing Touches

Picot Cast-off

This versatile edging can be used with almost any stitch. Worked in place of a conventional cast-off, it creates a decorative bumpy edge that looks attractive on all kinds of knitted items. Try it on the neckline of a jumper, for example, or on the brim of a hat, to edge a curtain tie-back or to create a border on a table mat.

To work picot cast-off:

This is used to cast off a multiple of three stitches, plus two.
Cast off 2 sts, *slip rem st from RH to LH needle, cast on 2 sts, cast off 4 sts; rep from * to end then fasten off rem st.

Lace Edging

This decorative border is worked lengthways. Simply keep repeating the eight-row stitch pattern until you have produced a lacy strip.

To work lace edging:

Cast on eight stitches.
Row 1 (WS): knit.
Row 2: sl1, k2, yfwd, k2tog, (yrn) twice, k2tog, k1. (9 sts)
Row 3: k3, p1, k2, yfwd, k2tog, k1.
Row 4: sl1, k2, yfwd, k2tog, k1, (yrn) twice, k2tog, k1. (10
Row 5: k3, p1, k3, yfwd, k2tog, k1.
Row 6: sl1, k2, yfwd, k2tog, k2, (yrn) twice, k2tog, k1. (11 s
Row 7: k3, p1, k4 yfwd, k2tog, k1.
Row 8: sl1, k2, yfwd, k2tog, k6.
Row 9: cast off 3 sts, k4, yfwd, k2tog, k1. (8 sts)

Rows 2–9 form the stitch pattern.

TIP The instruction (yrn) twice creates two extra stitch loops. Take care when working into these on the following row.

Garter Stitch Scallops

This simple border is worked lengthways, which means that you can keep knitting until it reaches the length you need. It can be used on knitted items such as blankets or curtain tie-backs, or stitched to items made from other fabric, such as curtains, towels, tablecloths and bedlinens.

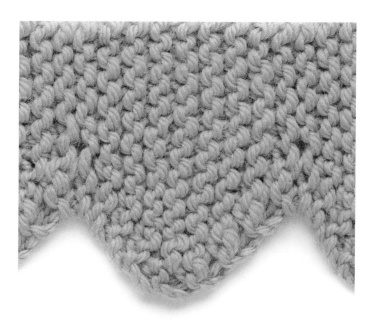

To work garter stitch scallops:

Cast on seven stitches.
Row 1: sl1, k3, kfb, k2. (8 sts)
Row 2: k1, kfb, k6. (9 sts)
Row 3: sl1, k5, kfb, k2. (10 sts)
Row 4: k1, kfb, k8. (11 sts)
Row 5: sl1, k7, kfb, k2. (12 sts)
Row 6: k1, kfb, k10. (13 sts)
Row 7: sl1, k9, kfb, k2. (14 sts)
Row 8: k1, kfb, k12. (15 sts)
Row 9: sl1, k to end.
Row 10: knit.
Row 11: sl1, k11, k2tog, k1. (14 sts)
Row 12: k1, skpo, k11. (13 sts)
Row 13: sl1, k9, k2tog, k1. (12 sts)
Row 14: k1, skpo, k9. (11 sts)
Row 15: sl1, k7, k2tog, k1. (10 sts)
Row 16: k1, skpo, k7. (9 sts)
Row 17: sl1, k5, k2tog, k1. (8 sts)
Row 18: k1, skpo, k5. (7 sts)

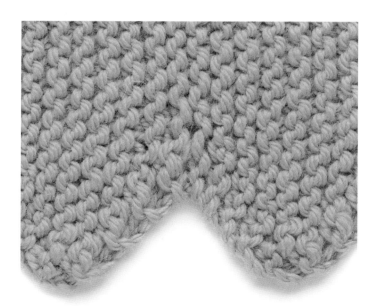

Rows 1–18 form the stitch pattern; repeat these rows until the work is the desired length, then cast off the remaining stitches.

TIP **Slipping the first stitch on odd-numbered rows helps to create a firm, neat straight edge.**

Point Edging

This pretty pointed border is easy to make and grows very quickly; make it any length you like. Similar in construction to the garter stitch scallops on the previous page, this edging is worked lengthways and has the potential for similar applications. Knit a long length of it to trim a knitted blanket or shawl, or stitch it on to a cotton or linen tablecloth or the inner edges of a pair of curtains, for example.

To work point edging:

Cast on six stitches.
Row 1 (RS): knit.
Row 2: yfwd, k2, k2tog, yfwd, k2. (7 sts)
Row 3: knit.
Row 4: yfwd, k to last 4 sts, k2tog, yfwd, k2. (8 sts)
Row 5: knit.
Row 6: as row 4. (9 sts)
Row 7: knit.
Row 8: as row 4. (10 sts)
Row 9: knit.
Row 10: as row 4. (11 sts)
Row 11: knit.
Row 12: cast off 5 sts, k1, k2tog, yfwd, k2. (6 sts)

Rows 1–12 form the stitch pattern; repeat these rows until the work is the desired length, then cast off the remaining stitches.

Petal Point Edging

This pointed is knitted lengthways and can be made any length you wish. It would be a good finishing touch around the edges of a knitted blanket but can also be added to non-knitted items such as towels and curtains, or used as a shelf edging.

To work petal point edging:

Cast on seven stitches.

Row 1 (WS): knit.
Row 2: sl1, k1, yfwd, k2tog, yfwd, k3. (8 sts)
Row 3: knit.
Row 4: sl1, k1, yfwd, k2tog, yfwd, k4. (9 sts)
Row 5: knit.
Row 6: sl1, k1, yfwd, k2tog, yfwd, k5. (10 sts)
Row 7: knit.
Row 8: sl1, k1, yfwd, k2tog, yfwd, k6. (11 sts)
Row 9: knit.
Row 10: sl1, k1, yfwd, k2tog, yfwd, k7. (12 sts)
Row 11: knit.
Row 12: sl1, k1, yfwd, k2tog, yfwd, k8. (13 sts)
Row 13: knit.
Row 14: sl1, k1, yfwd, k2tog, yfwd, k9. (14 sts)
Row 15: knit.
Row 16: sl1, k1, yfwd, k2tog, yfwd, k10. (15 sts)
Row 17: cast off 8 sts, k to end. (7 sts)

Rows 2–17 form the stitch pattern; repeat these rows until the work is the desired length, then cast off the remaining stitches.

Bell Edging

This fluted edging can be used on the edge of a jumper or jacket to create a little peplum. It would also look effective as a decorative border for the ends of a scarf. Note that, as the work progresses, you reduce the number of stitches, finishing with a third of the number you cast on.

To work bell edging:

Cast on a multiple of 12 stitches plus three, using a two-needle method.

Row 1 (RS): p3, *k9, p3; rep from * to end.
Row 2: k3, *p9, k3; rep from * to end.
Row 3: p3, *yb, skpo, k5, k2tog, p3; rep from * to end.
Row 4: k3, *p7, k3; rep from * to end.
Row 5: p3, *yb, skpo, k3, k2tog, p3; rep from * to end.
Row 6: k3, *p5, k3; rep from * to end.
Row 7: p3, *yb, skpo, k1, k2tog, p3; rep from * to end.
Row 8: k3, *p3, k3; rep from * to end.
Row 9: p3, *yb, sl1, k2tog, psso, p3; rep from * to end.
Row 10: k3, *p1, k3; rep from * to end.
Row 11: p3, *k1, p3; rep from * to end.
Row 12: as row 10.

Rows 1–12 form the stitch pattern.

TIP If you wish to add the edging to an item by sewing it in place, complete the 12 rows of the pattern, then cast off. Otherwise, do not cast off after row 12 but carry on knitting, using your main stitch – such as the stocking stitch used in the example shown here.

TIP Use a two-needle cast on to create a nice firm edge.

Leaf Edging

This edging creates a decorative hem for a garment such as a skirt or sweater, or could be used on the cast-on edge of a scarf or throw.

To work leaf edging:

Cast on a multiple of 13 stitches, plus two.
Row 1 (RS): k1, *k2, skpo, sl2, k3tog, p2sso, k2tog, k2; rep from * to last st, k1.
Row 2: p4, *yrn, p1, yrn, p6; rep from * ending last rep p4 instead of p6.
Row 3: k1, yfwd, *k2, skpo, k1, k2tog, k2, yfwd; rep from * to last st, k1.
Row 4: p2, *yrn, p2, yrn, p3, yrn, p2, yrn, p1; rep from * to last st, p1.
Row 5: k2, *yfwd, k1, yfwd, skpo, k1, sl1, k2tog, psso, k1, k2tog, (yfwd, k1) twice; rep from * to last st, k1.
Row 6: purl.
Row 7: k5, *yfwd, sl2, k3tog, p2sso, yfwd, k7; rep from * ending last rep k5 instead of k7.
Rows 8–10: knit.

Continue in main stitch (in the sample shown here, stocking stitch).

Special abbreviations

p2sso   pass two slipped stitches over

Fan Edging

Worked lengthways over 14 stitches, this deep, fairly complex border has an attractive wavy edge. Make it as long as you wish and use it to edge a knitted blanket or a fabric item such as a curtain, bed sheet or tablecloth. It would also be perfect for a special project such as a christening shawl.

To work fan edging:

Cast on 14 stitches.
Row 1 (RS): knit.
Row 2: k2, yfwd, k2tog, k5, yfwd, k2tog, yfwd, k3. (15 sts)
Row 3: k1, yfwd, k2tog, k to end.
Row 4: k2, yfwd, k2tog, k4, (yfwd, k2tog) twice, yfwd, k3. (16 sts)
Row 5: as row 3.
Row 6: k2, yfwd, k2tog, k3, (yfwd, k2tog) three times, yfwd, k3. (17 sts)
Row 7: as row 3.
Row 8: k2, yfwd, k2tog, k2, (yfwd, k2tog) four times, yfwd, k3. (18 sts)
Row 9: as row 3.
Row 10: k2, yfwd, k2tog, k1, (yfwd, k2tog) five times, yfwd, k3. (19 sts)
Row 11: as row 3.
Row 12: k2, yfwd, k2tog, k1, k2tog, (yfwd, k2tog) five times, k2. (18 sts)
Row 13: as row 3.
Row 14: k2, yfwd, k2tog, k2, k2tog, (yfwd, k2tog) four times, k2. (17 sts)
Row 15: as row 3.
Row 16: k2, yfwd, k2tog, k3, k2tog, (yfwd, k2tog) three times, k2. (16 sts)
Row 17: as row 3.
Row 18: k2, yfwd, k2tog, k4, k2tog, (yfwd, k2tog) twice k2. (15 sts)
Row 19: as row 3.
Row 20: k2, yfwd, k2tog, k5, k2tog, yfwd, k2tog, k2. (14 sts)
Row 21: as row 3.

Rows 2–21 form the pattern; repeat these rows until the work is the desired length.

Square

This pattern makes a neat square patch. Make one to use as a basket liner, table mat or potholder.

To work a square:

Cast on 65 stitches.
Row 1 (RS): k32, s2k, k1, p2sso, k to end. (63 sts)
Row 2: knit.
Row 3: k31, s2k, k1, p2sso, k to end. (61 sts)
Row 4: knit.
Row 5: k30, s2k, k1, p2sso, k to end. (59 sts)
Row 6: knit.

Continue working like this, decreasing at the centre of each odd-numbered row. When only three stitches remain, work the last row as follows: s2, k1, p2sso. Cut the yarn, leaving a tail, and pull this up through the remaining stitch to fasten off.

TIP Make a number of squares using leftover yarn; join together for a cosy, colourful patchwork blanket.

Feather and Fan Edging

This wavy edging is easy and relatively quick to knit. Use it to create an attractive border of varying width simply by repeating the stitch pattern; you can also use this stitch to create an allover textured lace fabric.

To work feather and fan edging:

Cast on a multiple of 12 stitches, plus two.
Row 1 (RS): knit.
Row 2: purl.
Row 3: k1, (k2tog) twice, (yfwd, k1) four times, (k2tog) twice; rep from * to last st, k1.
Row 4: knit.

Rows 1–4 form the pattern; repeat these rows until the work is the desired depth.

TIP Each pattern repeat forms a wavy garter stitch ridge. When your edging is the required depth, you can continue in stocking stitch, as shown in this example.

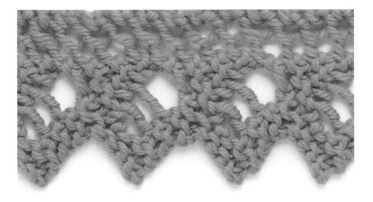

Chevron Edging

Worked lengthways, simply keep repeating the stitch pattern until your decorative narrow edging is the desired length.

To work chevron edging:

Cast on seven stitches.
Row 1 (RS): k2, yfwd, k2tog, (yfwd) twice, k2tog, k1. (8 sts)
Row 2: k3, p1, k2, yfwd, k2tog.
Row 3: k2, yfwd, k2tog, k1, (yfwd) twice, k2tog, k1. (9 sts)
Row 4: k3, p1, k3, yfwd, k2tog.
Row 5: k2, yfwd, k2tog, k2, (yfwd) twice, k2tog, k1. (10 sts)
Row 6: k3, p1, k4, yfwd, k2tog.
Row 7: k2, yfwd, k2tog, k6.
Row 8: cast off 3 sts, k4, yfwd, k2tog. (7 sts)

Rows 1–8 form the pattern; repeat these rows until the work is the desired length.

Ruffle Edging

This frilled edging can be used as the hem, cuffs or neckline on a sweater or cardigan, or as the ends of a scarf. It can be knitted as a fancy cast-on, continuing with your own choice of main stitch, or made as a trim, to be added to other items.

To work ruffle edging:

Cast on a multiple of four stitches, plus one.
Row 1 (RS): k1, *k2, pass first st on RH needle over the second and off the needle; rep from * to end.
Row 2: p1, *p2tog; rep from * to end.
Rows 3 and 4: knit.

Cast off, or continue with main stitch.

TIP Calculate the number of stitches to cast on as follows: multiply the number of stitches needed for the main piece by four, then subtract three.

Fringed Edging

This edging is worked lengthways. Use it to trim rugs, blankets or shawls. It can also be used on hems, yokes and sleeves.

To work fringed edging:

Cast on 14 stitches, using the thumb method.
Row 1 (RS): k2, yfwd, k2tog, k10.
Row 2: p9, k2, yfwd, k2tog, k1.

Rows 1 and 2 form the pattern; when the work is the desired length, cast off the first five stitches knitwise. Cut the yarn, leaving a tail, and fasten off by drawing it through the stitch on the right-hand needle. Drop the remaining stitches from the left-hand needle and unravel them to form the fringe. Cut through the loops at the ends, then knot the strands in groups of four, close to the knitted band.

Bobble Edging

A fancy edging like this can add texture and interest to an otherwise plain item. Use it on the hem and cuffs of a child's sweater or on the borders of a blanket.

To work bobble edging:

Cast on a multiple of six stitches, plus five.
Rows 1 and 2: knit.
Row 3: k5, *MB, k5; rep from * to end.
Rows 4–6: knit.

Cast off or continue in main stitch.

Special abbreviations

See Bobble Stitch, page 53, for abbreviations.

Circle

This plain knitted circle can be used to make table mats or a basket liner. It can also be used for the crown for a hat, knitted from the top downwards: once the circle is the desired size, just keep knitting straight with no additional shaping. The finished circle curls up at the edges and may need to be blocked.

To work a circle:

Cast on eight stitches and distribute these between four double-pointed needles, using the fifth to knit with.

Round 1: knit.
Round 2: kfb in each st. (16 sts)
Rounds 3–5: knit.
Round 6: kfb in each st. (32 sts)
Rounds 7–11: knit.
Round 12: kfb in each st. (64 sts)
Rounds 13–19: knit.
Round 20: *k1, kfb; rep from * to end of round. (96 sts)
Rounds 21–25: knit.
Round 26: *k2, kfb; rep from * to end of round. (128 sts)
Rounds 27–31: knit.
Round 32: *k3, kfb; rep from * to end of round. (160 sts)

Continue, knitting five rounds without increases then working an increase on the sixth round. In this way, you would knit rounds 33–37, then round 38 would be a repeat of k4, kfb, increasing the stitch count to 192; round 44 would be a repeat of k5, kfb, ending with a stitch count of 224; round 50 would be a repeat of k6, kfb, ending with a stitch count of 256, and so on.

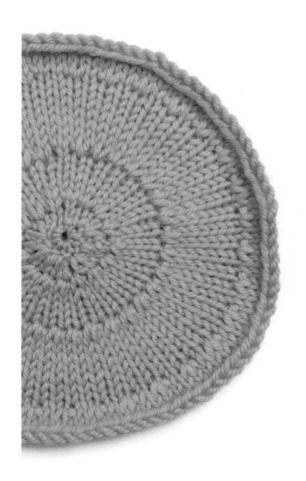

TIP **Knitting with five needles can be tricky for the first few rounds but, once you have more stitches on each needle, it becomes easier.**

Diamond Edging

Here is another useful border that is worked lengthways, allowing you to make it as short or as long as you wish. Your choice of yarn will affect the appearance of the finished edging, with a chunky yarn being suitable for edging a blanket or heavy curtain, a fine yarn for a shawl, or a medium-weight cotton yarn for a shelf edging or towel border.

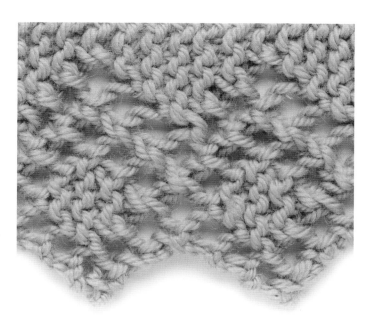

To work diamond edging:

Cast on nine stitches.
Row 1 (RS): knit.
Row 2: k3, k2tog, yfwd, k2tog, (yfwd, k1) twice. (10 sts)
Row 3: knit.
Row 4: k2, (k2tog, yfwd) twice, k3, yfwd, k1. (11 sts)
Row 5: knit.
Row 6: k1, (k2tog, yfwd) twice, k5, yfwd, k1. (12 sts)
Row 7: knit.
Row 8: k3, (yfwd, k2tog) twice, k1, k2tog, yfwd, k2tog. (11 sts)
Row 9: knit.
Row 10: k4, yfwd, k2tog, yfwd, k3tog, yfwd, k2tog. (10 sts)
Row 11: knit.
Row 12: k5, yfwd, k3tog, yfwd, k2tog. (9 sts)

Rows 1–12 form the pattern; repeat these rows until the work is the desired length, then cast off the remaining stitches.

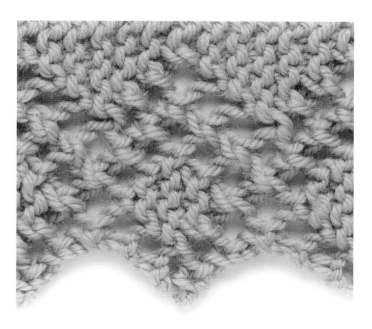

Hexagon

You could make a number of these and stitch them together, side by side, to make a patchwork blanket or throw. Or you could just make one large one, using a chunky yarn, and keep going until it is large enough for a rug or table cover. Whatever you choose to make, you may need a bit of practice getting to grips with manipulating four double-pointed needles but, once you have got the hang of this, the pattern is very straightforward.

To work a hexagon:

Cast on 12 stitches and distribute these between three double-pointed needles, using a fourth to knit with.

Round 1: knit.
Round 2: (yfwd, k2) six times. (18 sts)
Round 3: knit.
Round 4: (yfwd, k2) six times. (24 sts)
Round 5: knit.
Round 6: (kfb, k3) six times. (30 sts)
Round 7: knit.
Round 8: (kfb, k4) six times. (36 sts)

Continue working in this way, increasing six stitches on each even numbered round, until the hexagon is the desired size. Cast off knitwise.

TIP Place a marker at the beginning of each round, to keep track of where you are. A stitch counter may also help.

Octagon

Shapes like this, knitted in the round – such as the circle (see page 122) and hexagon (see opposite) – are called medallions. You can create seamless shapes; one of the most practical uses for these is as a hat crown. Depending on your choice of yarn, this octagon would also make a useful basket liner or table mat. A much larger version, knitted in a fine yarn, would also make a lovely shawl.

To work an octagon:

Cast on eight stitches and distribute these between four double-pointed needles, using a fifth to knit with.

Round 1: knit.
Round 2: kfb in each st. (16 sts)
Round 3: knit.
Round 4: (k1, kfb) eight times. (24 sts)
Round 5: knit.
Round 6: (k2, kfb) eight times. (32 sts)
Round 7: knit.
Round 8: (k3, kfb) eight times. (40 sts)
Round 9: knit.
Round 10: (k4, kfb) eight times. (48 sts)
Round 11: knit.
Round 12: (k5, kfb) eight times. (56 sts)
Round 13: knit.

Cast off knitwise.

TIP You could make a larger octagon than the one shown here by continuing the pattern in the way it has been set, adding eight stitches on every round. So, you would knit every odd-numbered round, then make two evenly spaced increases on each of the four needles on every even-numbered round until your octagon was the desired size.

I-cord

This is a very useful stitch technique, creating a neat, rounded cord, like a fine tube of knitting, that can have many useful applications. Make it any length you wish and use it to create ties, drawstrings loops and handles. It could even be the stalk for a knitted flower.

To work an I-cord:

Using two double-pointed needles, cast on two, three, four or five stitches, depending on how thick you wish the cord to be.
Row 1: *knit all stitches; slide the stitches from one end of the needle to the other; rep from *.

Row 1 forms the pattern; just keep repeating until the I-cord is the desired length.

TIP Tug the working yarn across the back of the stitches before you knit the next row, to keep the tension even.

Bobble Button

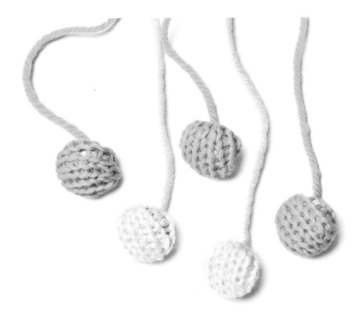

Knitted bobbles are a useful way of making buttons; they can also be used to embellish knitted pieces, perhaps in clusters.

To work a bobble button:

Cast on five stitches.
Row 1: knit.
Row 2: purl.

Rep rows 1 and 2 twice more, then row 1 again. Slip each stitch in turn over the first stitch and off the needle. Cut the yarn, leaving a long tail; thread through the remaining stitch to fasten off.

Thread a tapestry needle with the tail of yarn and sew a running stitch around the edge of the knitted piece. Pull up tightly, then secure. Leave the tail for attaching the bobble to the knitted item.

TIP When finishing the bobble, before you pull up the yarn tail to gather the edges, fill the bobble with a little stuffing or place a button inside.

Index

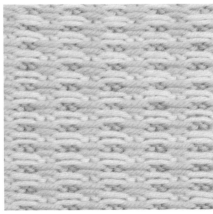

First published 2023 by
Guild of Master Craftsman Publications Ltd
Castle Place, 166 High Street, Lewes,
East Sussex, BN7 1XU, UK

ISBN 978-1-78494-666-1

A catalogue record for this book is available from the British Library.

Publisher **Jonathan Bailey**
Production **Jim Bulley**
Senior Project Editor **Sara Harper**
Editor **Nicola Hodgson**
Design Manager **Robin Shields**
Designer **Rhiann Bull**
Photography **Andrew Perris**
Illustrations **Simon Rodway**

Colour origination by GMC Reprographics
Printed and bound in China

To place an order, contact:
GMC Publications Ltd, Castle Place,
166 High Street, Lewes, East Sussex,
BN7 1XU, United Kingdom
Tel: +44 (0)1273 488005
www.gmcbooks.com